MULTI-FEATURES OF EDUCATION

MULTI-FEATURES OF EDUCATION

By

Dr. S.K. Panneer Selvam
Assistant Professor
Deptt. of Education
Bharathidasan University
Tiruchirappalli
Tamil Nadu

DISCOVERY PUBLISHING HOUSE PVT. LTD.
NEW DELHI-110 002

Published by:

Tilak Wasan

DISCOVERY PUBLISHING HOUSE PVT. LTD.
4831/24, Ansari Road, Prahlad Street
Darya Ganj, New Delhi-110002 (India)
Phone: +91-11-23279245, 43764432
Fax: +91-11-23253475
E-mail: parul.wasan@gmail.com
info@discoverypublishinggroup.com
web: www.discoverypublishinggroup.com

***First Edition:* 2011**
ISBN: 978-81-8356-712-1

Multi-Features of Education

Printed at:
Shree Balaji Art Press
Delhi

Preface

Well thought out educational policies (both academic and technical), schemes and projects and proper and prompt implementation of them with a missionary zeal decide the growth of the knowledge of a state or nation, development of a country is the function of human knowledge and skills imparted in institutions. The end value of any stream of education is all mind development of human resources which in turn is the development of a nation. Across the world a number of persons connected with education are doing researches on current problems to find out solutions. To widen the dimensions of education multilevel researches with an eye on future prospects and visions is inevitable. So with an idea to discriminate the knowledge acquired by M.Phil (Education) students, these educations are brought out. This edition is mainly a sum total of research works and the findings M.Phil (Education) students. The originality of this edition owes to the originality of the contributed presentations and research papers submitted by the M.Phil (Education) students. As an editor I acknowledged all the contributors.

Dr. S.K. Panneer Selvam

Contents

1

Environmental Attitudes of Students

ABSTRACT

In recent decades, two distinctive but interactive processes have severely affected the environment; the depletion of the natural resource base and the increasing appropriation of what are available for the benefit of a few. The rich pollute due to the wasteful overuse of resources and poor degrade the environment by surviving at its expense. At the same time, the demand for control and rights over common resources has been the reason for growing discontent and conflict in many countries. The increasing world population has further heightened environmental concerns and has given it a new urgency. Over the past twenty years environmental problems commands the attention of governments and public alike. The Delor's Commission Report *(Delors 1996)* states that "While humankind is increasingly aware of the threats facing its natural environment, the resources needed to put matters right have not yet been allocated, despite a series of international meetings, such as the UNCED, held in Rio de Janeiro in 1992, and despite the serious warnings of natural disasters or major industrial accidents. The truth is that all-out economic growth can no longer be viewed as the ideal way of reconciling material progress with equity, respect for the human condition and respect for the natural assets that we have a duty to hand on in good condition to future generations." An attitude is a disposition to react positively or negatively to some object. Attitudes are thought to be the predictors of behaviour. Gordon Allport (1935) called the attitudes the most indispensable concept in social psychology as they are thought to direct the behaviour. Thus understanding the attitudes will be of great importance to predict behaviour. Environmental Attitudes reflect an individual's preferences and values. Pollution, wildlife, extinction of species, natural resources, etc may be considered under the aegis of environmental concern. Measurement of the environmental attitudes of people, particularly young children is important in environmental education and implementation of any environmental programmes. This paper discusses the environmental attitudes of children in the age group of 12-17.

Environmental Attitudes Scale

Attitudes about the environment have been measured at different levels of specificity. Some studies have looked at broad environmental concern, while others have focussed on specific components of concern for nature and the environment (e.g., concern specifically for animals). Attitudes about the environment reflect an individual's preferences and values. Pollution, wildlife, extinction of species, natural resources, etc may be considered under the aegis of environmental concern. Kellert, a famous environmentalist, defined the typology from a set of human attitudes about nature, which he empirically tested by creating attitude scales. He investigated human attitudes toward nature, refining a typology of nine values that are thought to reflect a range of physical, emotional, and intellectual expressions of the tendency to associate with nature.

The present study is dealing with nature, and environment. The investigator constructed an Environmental Attitude Scale. Each of the seven attitude domains was standardized on a 0-1 scale. The individual attitude statement items were developed that fit within Kellert's seven attitude categories; moralistic, humanistic, naturalistic, ecologistic/scientific, dominionistic, utilitarian, and negativistic (Annexure). The number of items in each domain was limited to 3 to 4. By conducting item analysis, 28, 5-point Likert scale items were selected. The positive items were credited with 1=Strongly Disagree, 2=Disagree, 3=Undecided/Neither Agree Nor Disagree, 4= Agree, 5= Strongly Agree. The scoring was reversed for those items which were worded negatively, i.e., 1=Strongly Agree, 2= Agree, 3= Undecided / Neither Agree nor disagree, 4 = Disagree, and 5= Strongly Disagree. All items in a domain for each case (participant) were summed. This number was divided by the maximum possible value for that particular attitude domain (e.g., 16 for a 4-item domain). This standardized score was used for further analysis.

It was validated by experts and the reliability coefficient Cronbach's Alpha was found out to be *0.8257*. It was not reflecting the essence of the attitudes related to Nature in anyway.

The Study

In the present experiment, all the children in the age group 11-17, studying in schools are considered to be the population. 240 children from the schools in and around Chennai are selected as the sample by random sampling method. The sample was categorized into various sub-groups on the basis of various category variables. Age, Gender, Parental income, Parental profession, TV watching habits and Time spent in nature are the category variables used in the present study. In each category were further divided into sub-categories. The environmental attitude scale was administered into them and the total scores were collected. They are given below.

Table 1.1. The Mean and Standard Deviations of the Environmental Attitude Scores of the Sub-groups of the Sample

Variable	Category	Mean	Standard Deviation
Gender	Male	0.5314	0.0696
	Female	0.5285	0.0766
Age	12-13	0.5544	0.091
	14-15	0.5234	0.0713
	16-17	0.5269	0.0651
Type of School	Matriculation	0.5410	0.0767
	State Board	0.5104	0.0667
	CBSE	0.5387	0.0724
Food Habits	Vegetarian	0.5338	0.0704
	Non-Vegetarian	0.5282	0.0743
Place of Living	Rural	0.5361	0.0755
	Urban	0.5208	0.0710
ParentalIncome	Low Income	0.5223	0.0714
	Middle Income	0.5364	0.0716
	Upper Middle Income	0.5316	0.0798
	High Income	0.5368	0.0755
Parental Profession	Agriculture	0.5516	0.0622
	Service	0.5406	0.0788
	Business	0.5230	0.0745
	Daily Wages	0.5210	0.0721
	Others	0.5204	0.0663
Time spent in Nature	Rarely	0.5210	0.0642
	Few times per month	0.5277	0.0879
	1-2 times per week	0.5310	0.0766
	3-5 times per week	0.5347	0.0654
	Every Day	0.5437	0.0693
Watching TV programmes related to nature	Occasionally	0.5186	0.0837
	Few hours per month	0.5263	0.0533
	Less than 1 hour per day	0.5375	0.0747
	1-2 times per week	0.5634	0.0746
	2-4 hours daily	0.5409	0.0725

Descriptive Analysis

From Table 1.1, it is clear that there are slight variations in the environmental attitudes of the sub groups of the sample.

1. As far as Age group is concerned, the mean score of the age group (12-13) is *0.5544*, that of the (14-15) age group is *0.5234* and that of the age group (16-17) is *0.5269*. The attitude score is the highest for the lower age group and it decreases as the age increases. This means that the younger children are more pro-environmental than the elder ones.
2. As far as the Gender is concerned, the males have secured a mean score of *0.5314* whereas the females have scored *0.5285*, which is slightly less than that of males. That implies that the boys are more pro-environmental than the girls.
3. As far as the type of school is concerned, the Matriculation Board students have scored *0.5410* which is the highest, followed by the CBSE students with a score of *0.5387* and the State Board students secured *0. 5104*. It means that the Matriculation Board students are more environmental conscious than their counterparts.
4. In the case of the location of the sample, the rural students have higher pro-environmental attitudes with a score of *0.5361* and the city students are having only *0.5208*.
5. As far as food habits are concerned, the vegetarians have more pro-environmental attitudes with a score of *0.5338* and the non-vegetarians having *0.5282*. It is obvious that the vegetarians, due to their food habits, prefer to save the nature than the non-vegetarians.
6. In the case of the parental income is concerned, the middle income group and the high income group have secured *0.5364* and *0.5368* respectively. This is followed by the upper middle income group with *0.5316* and

the lower income group with *0.5223*. Generally, the lower income group is less environmental due to the hardships it faces. Here also, it is so. The higher and middle income groups are having more pro-environmental attitudes.

7. In the case of parental profession is concerned, the agricultural group is more environmental friendly with *0.5516* followed by the service group and the business group with *0.5406* and *0.5230*. The daily wages and the other group have obtained *0.5210* and *0.5204* respectively. It is obvious that the agriculture people are more pro-environmental than the others.
8. In the case of the time spent in nature, it is those who spent many hours per week who have the highest score of *0.5437* followed by the high spending students with *0.5347*. The moderates have scored *0.5310*. The other groups of low and very low are scoring *0.5277* and *0.5209* respectively. This means that the more the students spend time with nature, the more environmental conscious they become.
9. In the case of the Time spent in watching nature related programmes are concerned, those who are watching the natural programmes in TV 1-2 times per week have the highest score with 0.5634. This is followed by those who watch 1-2 hours daily with a score of 0.5409. The other groups have scored fewer score than these two groups.

Inferential Analysis: To further analyse the individual differences in the Environmental Attitudes of the sample sub-groups, the inferential statistics were conducted. The results are given below:

From Table 1.2, it is understood that there are not much statistical differences between the sub groups of the sample, except the type of school. To find out which sub groups are differing, Scheffe's post hoc analysis test has been conducted. The results are given in Table-1.3.

Table 1.2. The Significance between the Mean Environmental Attitude Scores of the Sub-groups of the Sample

Variable	'F' Value	Signi-ficance	Signi-ficance
Age Group	2.712	0.068	N.S.
Gender	0.096	0.757	N.S.
Type of School	4.468	0.012	Sig.
Location	2.506	0.115	N.S.
Food Habits	0.221	0.802	N.S.
Parental Income	0.433	0.730	N.S.
Parental Profession	1.252	0.290	N.S.
Times spent in Nature	0.387	0.818	N.S.
TV watching habits	1.718	0.147	N.S.

Table 1.3. The Significance between the Mean Environmental Attitude Scores of the Sub-groups of the Sample

	Sub-Groups	Significance Value	Signi-ficance
Matriculation	State Board	0.029	Sig.
Matriculation	CBSE	0.079	N.S.
State Board	Matriculation	0.029	Sig.
State Board	CBSE	0.047	Sig.
CBSE	Matriculation	0.079	N.S.
CBSE	State Board	0.047	Sig.

From Table-1.3, it is clear that there are significance differences between the Matriculation Board students and State Board students. Similarly, there are significant differences between the State Board students and the CBSE students. But there are not many differences between the Matriculation Board students and CBSE students.

Conclusion

From the present study, it is found that the younger children are having pro-environmental attitudes. On an average, the scores range from 0.51 to 0.56. This means that their environmental attitudes are around 56 per cent. It is the duty of the teachers and those who are interested in preserving nature to improve the scores of these children above 75 per cent. The environmental attitudes scores are very important in the context of any environmental programme or plan. By using proper teaching strategies and aids, the teachers should infuse the pro-environmental attitudes into the young children. As Delors Commission has stated, "We have a responsibility of handing over the earth in a better living condition to the future generations".

REFERENCES

1. Fishbein, M. (1963). An Investigation of the Relationships Between Beliefs About an Object and the Attitude Toward that Object. *Human Relations* 16:233-40.266.
2. Kellert, S.R. (1991). Japanese Perceptions of Wildlife. *Con.Bio,* 5:297-308.
3. Kellert, S.R. (1993). Attitudes, Knowledge, and Behavior Toward Wildlife Among the Industrial Superpowers: United States, Japan, and Germany. *Journal of Social Issues,* 49:53-69.
4. Kellert, S.R. (1995). Managing for Biological and Sociological Diversity, or 'deja vu, all over again. *Wild.Soc.Bull,* 23:274-278.
5. Rolston, H. (1985). Valuing Wild Lands. *Environmental Ethics,* 7:23-48.
6. Van Liere, K.D. and Dunlap, R.E. (1981). Environmental Concern: Does It Make a Difference How It's Measured. *Environmental Behaviour.* 13:651-76.
7. Williams, S.M. and McCrorie, R. (1990). The Analysis of Ecological Attitudes in Town and Country. *Journal of Environmental Management,* 31:157-62.

Appendix
Attitudes Towards Natural Environment

Please indicate how much you agree or disagree with each of the following statements. Please remember that we are looking for your general impressions. (Circle one number for each statement).

1. Strongly agree **2**. Agree **3.** Neither agree nor disagree **4**. Disagree **5**. Strongly disagree

01	All life forms found in nature have a right to live like humans	1	2	3	4	5
02	We have a moral responsibility to protect nature	1	2	3	4	5
03	It is cruel to keep birds and animals in captivity	1	2	3	4	5
04	Laboratory experiments on animals should be stopped	1	2	3	4	5
05	Most animals have feelings and thoughts as we have	1	2	3	4	5
06	I like pet animals very much	1	2	3	4	5
07	I don't understand how people should love nature	1	2	3	4	5
08	I have a deep affection for nature	1	2	3	4	5
09	I should help the animals when they are in trouble	1	2	3	4	5
10	The rich variety of plants and animals in nature is amazing	1	2	3	4	5
11	It is a waste of time to visit a forest for watching wildlife.	1	2	3	4	5
12	Nature provides me with inspiration and peace.	1	2	3	4	5

13	Nature supports all life on the globe	1	2	3	4	5
14	I wish to learn how species coexist and useful to each other	1	2	3	4	5
15	It is interesting to learn how nature functions	1	2	3	4	5
16	I feel bored to study how animals adapt to their surroundings	1	2	3	4	5
17	It is amazing to know the interaction between living and Non-living things	1	2	3	4	5
18	People can disturb nature, as they like	1	2	3	4	5
19	There is no need for hunting for managing wildlife.	1	2	3	4	5
20	Hunting is a challenge, which I enjoy	1	2	3	4	5
21	People should strictly control the natural environment Near where they live.	1	2	3	4	5
22	Natural environments managed by people are better than the Pristine ones.	1	2	3	4	5
23	The most important natural species are the ones, which give Us some useful products	1	2	3	4	5
24	Industries are necessary, even though they may harm the Environment.	1	2	3	4	5
25	Destroying natural habitats endangers the services, nature provides	1	2	3	4	5
26	Dangerous animals and plants should not exist	1	2	3	4	5
27	The world would not suffer, if some poisonous creatures Were eliminated	1	2	3	4	5
28	If I go to a forest, I will get hurt	1	2	3	4	5

2

Environmental Awareness for Teacher Educators

Introduction

"The earth provides enough to satisfy every person's need but not every person's need." —*Mahatma Gandhi*

Throughout history, mankind has adapted to the natural variation of the earth's system and its climate. Until very recently in the history of the earth, humans and their activities have not featured as a significant force in the dynamics of the earth system . But today, mankind has begun to match and even surpass the forces of nature in changing the earth system process.

Human population and the economic wealth of the world have grown rapidly over the past two centuries. These two factors have increased resource consumption significantly evident in agriculture and food production, industrial development, energy production and urbanization.

Definitions

Environment is derived from French word ' Environner" which means to encircle or surround. All the biological and non – biological things surrounding an organism are thus included in environment. Thus environment is sum total of water, air, and land, inter-relationships among themselves and also with the human beings, other living organisms and property (Environment Protection Act, 1986). The above definition clearly indicates that environment includes all the physical and biological surroundings and their interactions. Thus, in order to study the environment, one needs knowledge inputs from various disciplines such as life science to understand the biotic component and their interactions, physical and chemical structure of the abiotic components and every transfer of energy flow. Statistics and computer science serve as effective tools in environment modelling. Subjects like education, economics and sociology deal with socio-economic aspect associated with various development activities.

Concept of Environmental Awareness

Environmental awareness may be developed by identifying, analyzing and understanding the needs and problems of an individual, social life, or national life. Environmental awareness may be developed as to help the social groups and individuals to gain to variety of experiences and acquire a basic understanding of environment and its associated problems.

Environmental awareness brings about desirable attitudinal changes about man's relationship with his natural and manmade surroundings. Environmental awareness is in fact essential for us. All of us want to live in a clean, healthy aesthetic, beautiful, safe and secure environment for a long time and wish to handover a clean and safe and earth to our future generations.

Statement of the Problem

In the study the investigator attempts to find out the environmental awareness among Student Teachers and Teacher Educators in Tamil Nadu.

Need and Significance of the Study

Every living being needs to survive. The basic needs come from air, water, soil and energy. The greatest challenge is to rediscover our place on this planet. Our inventions has enabled to overcome virtually any ecological barrier, hence we inhabit and exploit every part of the world.

Knowledge about the environment is not an end, but rather a beginning. It promotes attitudinal and behavioural change. Therefore, environmental awareness is an agent of change and a step towards community empowerment. So, the investigator felt the need of studying this aspect of environmental awareness among teacher trainees who would be at the forefront in pursuing the opportunities for professional training to incorporate the principles of sustainability in their courses.

Objectives of the Study

The main objectives of the study are:

1. To promote and develop environmental awareness among student teachers and Teacher educators
2. To evaluate the awareness among student teachers and teacher educators.
3. To compare the relations among categorical variables (gender, age, subject, marital status, community, annual income of the family and parents qualification) towards environment.

Sample

The student teachers and teacher educators in Tamil Nadu will form the population. Among this population, suitable sample will be selected by random sampling method depending upon the availability and necessity of the study.

Description of the Tool

Environmental awareness includes pollution in land, air, water, noise, various pollutants, general awareness and conserving natural resources. A suitable research tool will be prepared. The investigator will select a suitable methodology and research design. The tool may contain a detailed personal data to be filled in by the respondents regarding their gender, age, section, class and year of the study, martial status, and community, annual income of the parents and educational qualifications of the parents.

Data Analysis

The data collected will be analyzed keeping in mind the hypotheses to be tested. Suitable statistical tools will be used to analyze the data including inferential and descriptive statistical tools. The t-test, analysis of variance will be carried out to test the null hypothesis about the significant difference in means between two or more population and variables.

Time Schedule

- To find a problem and its consolidation 6 months
- To determine aim and methodology 6 months
- Tool designing, reliability, validity 6 months
- Conduction of the study 6 months
- Data collection and analysis 6 months
- Research report 6 months

Conclusion

In the present study it was found that educational qualification of parents has significant correlation on general and overall environmental awareness among student teachers and teacher educators. From the findings it is clear that education plays a major role in creating environmental awareness.

3

Gender Differences in Social Maturity

ABSTRACT

Every difference of environment means a difference in one's habit and one's way of living in so far as these differences create a different environment, a dynamic equilibrium of life is maintained through a processing of constant selections and constant adaptations. The society is not the world but is directly related to every one's life and maturity. The more complex the adaptation with society becomes, the more complex the social maturity of intelligence, maturity according to the need. Society is significant medium where certain quality of life and certain types of activity and occupation are provided with the aim of securing child's development based on the social needs. Since is a stem of growth characteristics of teacher trainees should adapt to the society which we live and to which he is expected to adjust and contribute, the social maturity receives importance at the present context. The conduct of many individual in the society tells about the trainees social maturity through which he can respond right according to the teaching situation. In this study, the author had selected a sample of 400 student teachers studying in various colleges in and around Chennai and found the significant differences in their Social Maturity according to their age, gender type of school, area, parental income, community and parental qualification. The data had been analysed with the help of ANOVA and other statistical methods and the results are obtained. The study found that there are significant differences in social maturity with respect to the categorical variables.

Social Maturity

Maturity assumes accountability, constantly assesses, judges and takes appropriate decisions. Maturity develops a balanced emotional outlook, helping the individual to accept himself, his talents and limitation and to accept others as they are. It analysis values and internalizes them consistently. It helps towards progressive advancement in spiritual growth, impelling the individual to adapt himself to change and to life without emotional crisis. Abraham Sperling (1967) defined social maturity in the following words, "An adolescent should get along with others. He ought to develop self-reliance in matter of taste and ought to develop tolerance of human differences". Nazarath Maria E. Waples (1978) defines as, "Maturity is the blossoming of man's character into a unified totality. It discerns the process that contributes to the psychological and physical growth and well being of man". Henry E. Garrett (1969) states "Social maturity is the degree of social participation as measured by child's activities, attitudes and play interests. It is related to physical growth and maturity and to mental ability. Every individual develops his own unique way of adjustment in the society. An individual, since his birth attempts to adjust to his environment". Henry.E. Garrett (1968) says, "Social maturity is the degree of social participation as measured by child's activities, attitudes and play interests. It is related to physical growth and maturity and to mental ability".

Stages of Social Maturity

An individual takes times in his social development. So, we may think of some stages of social maturity according to the physical, mental, emotional and language development of the individual. They are:

- Awareness of the presence of another person.
- Mixing with others
- Understanding of social relationships.

Understanding of all the above three things refers to human stages of social maturity.

Methodology

This study is taken to find out the significant differences in Social Maturity among the student teachers. The Dr.Nalini Rao tool has been taken for the study. It consists of various dimensions such as social maturity with words, age, gender type of school area; parental income, community and parental qualification are taken as the categorical variables. A sample of 400 student teachers studying in and around Chennai was taken as the sample. Stratified Random Sampling process was used. The following hypotheses were framed:

Hypotheses

1. There is a significant difference between male and female teacher trainees on their social maturity.
2. There is a significant difference between TTI and DIET teacher trainees on their social maturity.
3. There is a significant difference between teacher trainees belonging to nuclear and joint families on their social maturity.
4. There is a significant difference between teacher trainees from rural and urban area on their social maturity.
5. There is a significant difference of teacher trainees on their social maturity based on their parental income.

6. There is a significant difference on social maturity of teacher trainees based on their community.
7. There is no significant difference on social maturity of teacher trainees based on their father's qualification.
8. There is no significant difference on social maturity of teacher trainees based on their mothers qualification.
9. There is no significant difference on social maturity of teacher trainees based on their age.

Hypothesis-1

There is a significant difference between male and female teacher trainees on their social maturity.

The Table Showing the 't' value of Male and Female Teacher Trainees on their Social maturity

Variable	Gender	N	Mean	S.D	S.E.M	t - Value	L.S
Social	Male	100	203.46	23.645	2.364	4.617	0.01
Maturity	Female	300	214.58	19.859	1.147		

The calculated value of 't' 4.617 is greater than the table value, so there is significant difference occur at 0.01 levels. Thus the Hypothesis is accepted.

Hypothesis-2

There is a significant difference between TTI and DIET teacher trainees on their social maturity.

The Table showing the 't' Value of TTI and Diet Teacher Trainees on their Social Maturity

Variable	Ty.INS	N	Mean	S.D	S.E.M.	t - Value	L.S
Social	DIET	199	217.37	20.251	1.436	5.35	0.01
Maturity	Private	201	206.29	21.105	1.489		

The calculated value of "t" 5.35 is greater than the table value, so there is significant difference occur at 0.01 levels. Thus the Hypothesis is accepted.

Hypothesis-3

There is a significant difference between teacher trainees belonging to nuclear and joint families on their social maturity.

The Table Shwoing the 't' Value of Teacher Trainees belonging to Nuclear and Joint Families on their Social Maturity

Variable	Category	N	Mean	S.D	S.E.M.	t - Value	L.S
Social Maturity	Nuclear	211	215.53	22.749	1.566	3.74	0.01
	Joint	189	207.64	18.971	1.380		

The calculated value of 't' 3.74 is greater than the table value, so there is significant difference occur at 0.01 levels. Thus the Hypothesis is accepted.

Hypothesis-4

There is a significant difference between teacher trainees from rural and urban area on their social maturity.

The Table Shwoing the 't' Value of Teacher Trainees from Rural and Urban area on their Social Maturity

Variable	Category	N	Mean	S.D	S.E.M.	t - Value	L.S
Social Maturity	Social	214	216.42	20.239	1.383	4.750	0.01
	Urban	186	206.49	21.499	1.576		

The calculated value of 't' 4.75 is greater than the table value, so there is significant difference occur at 0.01 level. Thus the Hypothesis is accepted.

Hypothesis-5

There is a significant difference of teacher trainees on their Social Maturity based on their parental income.

The Table Shwoing the 't' Value of Teacher Trainees on their Social Maturity Based on their Parental Income

Variable	Category	N	Mean	S.D	S.E.M.	t - Value	L.S
Social Maturity	Low income	330	211.54	21.474	1.182	0.534	NS
	High income	70	213.04	21.094	2.521		

The calculated value of 't' (.534) is less than the table value, so there is not significant difference at 0.01 level. Thus the Hypothesis is rejected.

Hypothesis-6

There is a significant difference on social maturity of teacher trainees based on their community.

Anova Showing the Difference in Social Maturity of Teacher Trainees to Different Communities

Variable	S.V.	S.S	D.F	Mean	F	L.S
Social Maturity	Between Groups	4753.860	2	2376.930	5.308	0.01
	Within Groups	177793.54	397	447.843		
	Total	**182547.40**	**399**	—		

From the above table the calculated value of 'F' (5.308) is greater than the table value is significant difference at 0.01 level. Thus the Hypothesis is accepted.

Hypothesis-7

There is no significant difference on social maturity of teacher trainees based on their father's qualification.

Anova Showing the Difference in Social Maturity of Teacher Trainees Based on Father's Qualification

Variable	S.V.	S.S	D.F	Mean	F	L.S
Social Maturity	Between Groups	1865.813	2	932.907	2.050	N.S
	Within Groups	180681.58	397	455.117		
	Total	**182547.40**	**399**	—		

The calculated value of 'F' (2.050) is less than the table value is not significant difference at 0.01 level. Thus the Null Hypothesis is retained.

Hypothesis-8

There is no significant difference on social maturity of teacher trainees based on their mother qualification.

Anova Showing the Difference in Social Maturity of Teacher Trainees based on Mother's Qualification

Variable	S.V.	S.S	D.F	Mean	F	L.S
Social Maturity	Between Groups	3484.033	2	1742.016	3.862	0.05
	Within Groups	179063.36	397	451.041		
	Total	**182547.40**	**399**	—		

The calculated value of 'F' (3.862) is greater than the table value is significant difference at 0.05 level. Thus the null hypothesis is not accepted.

Hypothesis-9

There is no significant difference on social maturity of teacher trainees based on their age.

Anova Showing the Difference in Social Maturity of Teacher Trainees based on Different Age

Variable	S.V.	S.S	D.F	Mean	F	L.S
Social	Between Groups	1832.424	2	916.212		
Maturity	Within Groups	180714.97	397	455.201	2.013	NS
	Total	**182547.40**	**399**	—		

The calculated value of 'F' (2.013) is less than the table value is not significant difference at 0.01 levels. Thus the null hypothesis is retained.

Major Findings of the Study

The major findings are presented below:

1. It was found that significant difference exists on the social maturity of male and female teacher trainees.
2. It was found that significant difference exists on the social maturity of TTI and DIET students.
3. It was found that significant difference exists on the social maturity of teacher trainees from joint and nuclear family of the teacher trainees.
4. It was found that there is a significant difference between TTI and DIET teacher trainees with respect to their social maturity on the basis of their community.
5. It was found that there is a significant difference between TTI and DIET teacher trainees with respect to their social maturity on the basis of their urban and rural area.
6. It was found that there is no significant difference between TTI and DIET teacher trainees with respect to their social maturity on the basis of parental qualification.
7. It was found that there is no significant difference between TTI and DIET teacher trainees with respect to their social maturity on the basis of parental income.

8. It was found that there is no significant difference between TTI and DIET teacher trainees with respect to their social maturity on the basis of their age.
9. It was found that significant relationship exists between social maturity and components of TTI and DIET students.

Conclusion

Social maturity is an aspect that makes an individual adjusted to the society at large. It is related to the development of the personality of a student. Students studying in TTI and DIET are forced to adhere to institution regulations as well as social activities. We find that if the students fall in line with the social relationship system and obeying its regulations they may possess a higher social maturity. Therefore for teacher trainees social maturity is essential for their daily life to adopt the classroom situation. Hence, the study has a direct impact on the educational practice. The following are some of the major recommendations to be implemented for the social maturity of the students.

- Educators and Administrators should bring about awareness among students to give more importance to develop social maturity.
- In order to develop social maturity intensive training should be provided.

REFERENCE

1. Abraham Sperling (1967). *Definition of Social Maturity,* Vikas Publications, New Delhi.
2. Adhiesehiah, W.T.V. and Pavanasam, R. (1974). *Sociology in Theory and Practice,* Shanthi Publishers, New Delhi, p.38.
3. Agnihotri. L.S. (1991). Conducted *A Cross-cultural Comparative Study Between Tribal and Non-tribal First Generation and Traditional Learners in Relation to Their Social Maturity and Educational Adjustment,* M.Phil Thesis in Psychology.

4. Bauses Ann Leslie (1995). Measured the Effect of Participation in a Peer Facilitation Project on Sixth Grades Self Esteem, *Social Maturity and Patterns of Social Choice*. Ph.D. Kent State University.
5. Bhusan. A. (1994). Conducted *A Study Done on the Social Maturity Across Sex and Family Vocations*. Buch, M.B., The Educational Research, Volume II.
6. Ghosh S. (1975). *A Study of the Social Maturity of Bengali Children, Applied Psychology,* Calcutta University.
7. Pattraman Jempengern (1986). *Social Maturity of Higher Secondary Students in Thailand*, Dissertation Abstract International.
8. Henry I. Garrent (1968). *General Psychology.* Eurasia Publishing House Pvt. Ltd., New Delhi, p.88.
9. John W. Best (1977). *Research in Education,* Third Edition, Prentice Hall India Pvt. Ltd., New Delhi.
10. John W. Best and James V. Khan (1989). *Research in Education,* Prentice Hall (P) Ltd., New Delhi.

4

Creativity Differences of Teacher Trainees

ABSTRACT

Education is the fulcrum upon which hangs the peaceful evolutionary transition of Society. It plays a vital role in building a society. The term creativity is widely used with reference to the creative people, the creative process, even a creative environment. Creativity is the ability to produce work that is both novel and appropriate. However, environmental factors will interact with individual differences and influence the creative process. Amabile (1996) describes four phases in the creative process, namely: 1.Problem identification, 2.Preparation, 3.Response generation, and 4.Validation and communication. Creativity is best conceptualized not as a personality trait or as a general ability, but as a behaviour resulting from particular constellations of personal characteristics, cognitive abilities, and social environments. There is an assumption that there is a relationship between natural / social environment and creative thinking. Age, School, Gender, Fluency, Flexibility and Originality are found to be affecting creativity in children. In this study, the author had selected a sample of 225 student teachers studying in various colleges in and around Chennai and found the significant differences in their creativity according to their age, type of school, gender, fluency, flexibility and originality levels. The data had been analysed with the help of ANOVA and other statistical methods and the results are obtained. The study found that there are significant differences in creativity with respect to the categorical variables.

Creativity

The term creativity is widely used with reference to the creative people, the creative process, even a creative environment (Brown 1989). Our interest is in the process, culminating in a novel and effective solution to an open-ended problem. The importance of both novelty and effectiveness is reflected in the following definition. Creativity is the ability to produce work that is both novel and appropriate (Sternberg 1988). This definition is widely accepted in the creativity literature Guilford (1950) made an important contribution to our understanding of creativity when he distinguished between convergent and divergent thinking processes. Convergent thinking is similar to conventional notions of intelligence in which existing knowledge / information is synthesized to arrive at the single most appropriate answer. Guilford argued that creativity is expressed in terms of divergent thinking, however this led to measuring creativity in terms of the number of fundamentally different solutions that were generate Creativity was initially studied as an intellectual or personality trait. The emphasis was on the creative individual and the nature of creativity was considered to be a black box' (Barron and Harrington 1981). More recently, however, there have been various attempts to describe and model the creative process so that it can then be effectively managed.

Factors Influencing Creative Process

Amabile (1983) argues that creativity is best conceptualized not as a personality Trait or as a general ability, but as a behaviour resulting from particular constellations of personal characteristics, cognitive abilities, and social environments. This view was shared by most contemporary theorists (Mumford et.al 1993) who emphasize changing the environment in order to promote and facilitate creativity. It is particularly relevant for educators wishing to establish an environment that supports creativity by managing the factors that promote or inhibit it. Amabil's componential model of creativity specifically recognizes the importance of domain-relevant skills, motivation and creativity relevant skills.

Methodology

This study is taken to find out the significant differences in creativity among the student teachers. The Baquer Mehdi's Creativity tool has been taken for the study. It consists of various dimensions such as thinking cratively with words, problems, novel use of things, making things more interesting and useful, etc. The originality, flexibility and fluency are considered various dimensions of creativity. Age, gender and type of school are taken as the categorical variables. A sample of 225 student teachers studying in and around Chennai was taken as the sample. Stratified Random Sampling process was used. The following hypotheses were framed:

Hypotheses

1. There are no significant differences in fluency with respect to the age, gender and type of school.
2. There are no significant differences in flexibility with respect to the age, gender and type of school.
3. There are no significant differences in originality with respect to the age, gender and type of school.

Analysis

Hypothesis: 1

There are no differences in fluency with respect to the age, gender and type of schod:

Table 4.1. The results of the 't' test for the differences in fluency with respect to age, gender and type of school

Fluency	Variable	Class	N	Mean	S.D	S.E.M.	't'	Sig.
	Gender	Male	125	16.66	8.860	0.79	2.45	0.05
		Female	100	17.94	8.079	0.81		
	Age	Below-20	112	18.62	7.43	0.70	1.180	N.S
		Above-20	113	15.86	9.39	0.87		
	Type of School	Government	125	17.15	8.719	0.783	0.167	N.S
		Govt.Aided	100	17.34	8.326	0.828		

From Table 4.1, it is understood that there are no significant differences among the students in fluency as far as the age and type of schools are concerned. But in gender, there are some differences; the creativity of boys is 8.860, slightly higher that of the girls, i.e., 8.079.

Hypothesis: 2

There are no significant differences in flexibility with respect to the age, gender and type of school.

Table 4.2. The results of the 't' test for the differences in flexibility with respect to age, gender and type of school

Flexibility	Variable	Class	N	Mean	S.D	S.E.M.	't'	Sig.
	Gender	Male	125	1593	8.824	0.75	2.34	0.05
		Female	100	1835	6.746	0.68		
	Age	Below-20	112	1682	7.81	0.73	0.35	N.S
		Above-20	113	1719	7.81	0.73		
	Type of School	Government	125	1798	7.953	0.714	2.085	0.05
		Govt.Aided	100	1581	7.478	0.744		

From Table 4.2, it is understood that there are no significant differences among the students in flexibility as far as the age is concerned. But in gender, there are some differences; the creativity of boys is 8.824, slightly higher that of the girls, i.e., 6.746,and typeof school there are some differences the creativity of govt institution 7.953 slightly higher that of the Govt. Aided institution i.e.,7.478.

Hypothesis: 3

There are no significant differences in originality with respect to the age, gender and type of school.

Table 4.3. The results of the 't' test for the differences in originality with respect to age, gender and type of school

Orginality	Variable	Class	N	Mean	S.D	S.E.M.	't'	Sig.
	Gender	Male	125	18.86	7.326	0.66	2.94	0.01
		Female	100	15.85	7.921	0.80		
	Age	Below-20	112	17.38	7.71	0.72	0.29	N.S
		Above-20	113	17.68	7.77	0.73		
	Type of School	Government	125	16.68	7.712	0.695	1.814	N.S
		Govt.Aided	100	18.55	7.650	0.761		

From Table 4.3, it is understood that there are no significant differences among the students in orginality as far as the age and type of schools are concerned. But in gender, there are some differences; the creativity of girls is 7.921, slightly higher that of the boys, i.e., 7.326.

Findings

1. In fluency level there are significant differences among men and women. male member's scores higher than the female teacher trainees.
2. In flexibility, there are significant differences among male and female trainees. male member's scores higher than the female teacher trainees.
3. It was found that a significant difference occurred in the originality of men and women teacher trainees.
4. It was found that there was no significant difference in the fluency and originality level of teacher trainees studying in Government and Government Aided

Institutes. In the case of flexibility level significant difference was found among the teacher trainees.

5. It was found that there was no significant difference in the flexibility and originality level of teacher trainees studying low age-group and high age-group students. In the case of fluency level significant difference was found among the teacher trainees.

Conclusion

One of the objectives of carrying out this research is to arrive at specific conclusions. The aim of the present study was to study creativity of secondary grade teacher trainees. Creativity as something that is necessary for the discovery of creative solutions to problems. Solving problems is not just a scientific or engineering activity, even educationists are commissioned to express a concept or an idea in a certain way. What makes one solution creative and another simply ordinary. It seems that it is often the context within which a solution is offered that establishes creativity. This means that creativity is not simply a mental process. There may be little to distinguish creativity from expertise. Creative solutions are very much need for the problem in active society. It is very essential for the teacher trainees to train them to have a creative solution in the classrooms. The trainees become a good creative teacher. A creative teacher is sensitive to the problems arising either in the classrooms or in the school and has got the capacity to suggest more than one solution to solve these problems.

REFERENCES

1. BAQER MEDHI (1977) Creativity in Teaching and Learning, Mysore Regional College of Education.
2. DELLS, M and E.L.GAIER, (1970) Identification of Creativity, The Individual Psychology Bill.
3. GUILFORD J.P. (1950) Creativity, American Psychologist, McGraw Hill New York.

4. MACKINNON (1962) Fastering Creativity in Students of Engineering, J. Eng. Education.
5. STEIN,M.I (1974) Stimulating Creativity, Vol I, Individual Procedures, Academic Press, New York.
6. TORRANCE (1965) Rewarding Creativity Behaviour, Englewood Cliffs, W.J., Prentice Hall, New Delhi.
7. THIRUMURTHY S.P. (1987) A Study of Creative Thinking Abiligy of Secondary School Students in the context of some Psycho-socio Factors IV Survey of Research in Education 1983-88, Vol. I, p. 516-517.

5

e-Learning in ODL System

ABSTRACT

e-Learning system provides a synchronous or asynchronous multi-media delivery and enables a collaborative environment for sharing the knowledge. This is to provide virtual classrooms in a multi class/ multi-studio environment with seamless two way interaction between the students and teachers. The virtual studio environment is created and the remote virtual classrooms join any educational studio based on their choice of course/training sessions. Every e-learning environment consists of various components, viz., content management, portal management, e-learning management, library, studio management, exam management, knowledge management, etc. Each component has its own features, functions and limitations. Every e-learning environment differs in these features. This paper discusses the various components of an e-learning system which is suitable for an open and distance learning system, particularly in Tamil Nadu Open University.

Salient Features of e-Learning environment

The e-Learning environment has certain salient features. They are given below:

(*i*) It provides one to one, one to many and many too many connectivity through multicasting network and enables the remote virtual classrooms to interact and share knowledge.

(*ii*) It provides integrated chat services, message services, question and answer services, desktop sharing services, whiteboard services, Internet services and digital library services.

(*iii*) It captures all the live sessions into knowledge repository, so that it can be used for the review learning process.

(*iv*) It is scalable, reliable and robust.

(*v*) It provides learning experience to the students in their course work study, assignments, and integrated notebooks for their selected subject of study, project, quiz and laboratory experiments.

(*vi*) A question bank enables to conduct secured examination using digital signatures and cryptography techniques.

(*vii*) Content management system generates the content, enables the secured content workflow for approval and deployment for delivery of e-learning content and live lecture content.

(*viii*) Digital library provides the resources, books, materials and documents for universal access.

(*ix*) An integrated portal system encapsulating all the components acts as a single window interface for the students / teacher / system administrator.

(*x*) It provides integrative collaborative conferencing and meeting facility to enable VIPs, experts, faculty and students to collaborate among themselves or individually. This acts as a helpdesk to students for online support.

(*xi*) It provides a scalable system to multiple studio environments with similar set up from geographically dispersed locations through the inter linked broadband network. This enables the multi studio scheduling, managing multi studio operations from the central hub.

Types of e-learning Environments

There are the following three types of learning environments generally practiced:

- Synchronous Learning Environment
- Asynchronous Learning Environment
- Collaborative Conferencing Environment

Let us discuss these categories, their nature, functions and uses.

I. Synchronous Learning Environment

In synchronous learning environment, the teacher and students are interacting simultaneously. This needs efficient collaborative tools, a broadband connectivity, good quality audio-video systems and tele-communication networks. It includes the following collaborative tools.

- Synchronous delivery of live audio, video and data
- Presentation control system
- Permission handling
- Text chat and whiteboard
- Messaging service
- Queries and responses
- Audio and Video interaction
- Desktop sharing

- Digital library reference and interface
- Surfing and referencing through internet
- Online survey or polling

II. Asynchronous Learning Environment

This is specially designed for e-learning / review learning purpose. The following are the integrated module:

Portal Management System

It provides integrated access to all services and Tele-Education solutions by personalized login. This enables the students to access University information, Affiliated study centres, Courses, Result announcement, Exam schedule, News and Events, Photo gallery, Announcements, Flash News, Instant poll, Feedback and University Directory.

e-Learning Management System

It is an online learning solution and helps to automate the training and learning events among university, distance education study centres and students. This application registers monitors and captures data from study centres and provides consolidated reports to the university. It provides online learning experiences that allow students, faculties and administrators to achieve their educational goals.

Content Management

It facilitates the deployment of syllabus and the online course content over the web through dynamic workflow for verification, validation and approval for final deployment for the course content.

Digital Library

It provides the facility to upload, store, index, categorize, search and view the electronic books, journals, manuscripts in PTIF, PDF, RTF, and HTML formats.

Exam Management

Providing the facility of question paper generation, online and off-line exam and secured delivery of question papers with digital signatures and encryption.

Tele-education Knowledge Management

It captures the live lecture events and student-teacher interaction for review learning purpose at students' own convenience and pace. This will provide the recorded lecture events through web and simulates the live virtual classroom.

Studio Management

It is designed to administer the studio operations for the timetable schedule by fixing the course, lecture topic, time slot to the respective subject expert. It will be scalable to manage multiple studios in different location seamlessly in a virtually connected and network environment with different communication modes.

Working

The system provides a single window learning portal, which acts as an interface among learners, instructors and system administrators. It provides synchronized multi media delivery and provides a collaborative environment for sharing the knowledge.

The delivery framework has a thick client through VSAT/ Leased line / Broadband / Wi-MAX connectivity and Thin client with the same GUI through Internet with security mechanism. The teacher can give a presentation using PowerPoint slides with animation, flash animation, HTML, etc, and address the remote locations, interacts through various collaborative tools. He can refer the web pages; delegate the remote expert to give a lecture. It has an interface with the digital library, and can search for a particular page and push the page to all the participants.

There are many kinds of interaction in this system:

Student	-	Student
Student	-	Teacher
Student	-	Content
Teacher	-	Teacher
Teacher	-	Content
Content	-	Content

Servers

There are various servers used in this system. The following are some common servers used in this system:

Studio Control Server

It provides complete control and coordination in a cohesive manner among the participating remote virtual classrooms and teacher applications to deliver the contents and enables real time interaction. It takes care of the request handler services from various remote classrooms for joining the multicast group and from Agent server for joining and presenting the lecture section.

Video and Audio Streaming Server

It is suitably customized and integrated to this system and able to transmit live audio and video over IP networks. It receives live analog and digital signals from the teacher side, encode them in real time to MPEG – 1 over MPEG – 4 and stream them over an IP network in multicast or in unicast mode.

Presentation Capture Server

Through this server, content with text, power point slides, video clippings, multimedia, graphics, animation and drawings running in the teacher unit PC can be captures and encoded for transmission.

Collaboration Server

It runs within the studio control server. It addresses the chat and whiteboard communication across the agent and its clients. It provides the basic abstraction of a session. It supports multi point communication among connected application entities over the networks. It is an interface for the Internet URL.

Multimedia Recording Agent Server

All the daily proceedings of the live session are recorded and archived through this server for future telecast or review learning. It synchronizes the session with audio, video, and data together based on the timings as per the actual broadcast delivery of the session.

Features of the Teacher and Student Software

Teacher	Student
Presentation content	View presentation
Student list	Join
View questions	Leave
Message services	Ask question
View message	Audio chat request
Text chat	View reply
Shared Whiteboard	Sent / Receive message
Push to Whiteboard	Text chat
Speak	Shared Whiteboard
Return Video	Internet browsing
Internet Interface	
Digital Library Interface	
Enabling remote client as a teacher	
Desktop sharing	
Quiz	

Portal Management System

It is the gateway to all the administrators to get access to the web based applications. This help to administer and deploy administrative and learning activities. It allows students, parents, faculty, affiliates and administrators to achieve their academic events. This offers various services and technologies. It offers the following services:

- General information to the public and students about the institution, departments, courses offered, exam announcements and results
- Provides features and functions and access privileges appropriate to each user
- Consistent navigation and look and feel for all online educational programmes and support services
- Dynamic menu links in the home page and also necessary links to various reputed bodies with international and national importance
- Career opportunity details
- FAQ relevant to the study programmes
- Parent access facility to see students' profile, fees and performance
- Alumni access module for online registration of alumni, display of alumni list
- Announcement, flash news, and News and Events
- Instant poll to share students' view points
- Student discussion forum for collaboration
- Online registration at the students' interested learning centres
- Message desk for messages from general users

e-Learning System

It enables users to deliver and manage learning resources efficiently and cost effectively. It helps and automates the administration of training and learning events by creating a suitable platform to achieve effective e-learning with the standards of SCORM conformance. To meet the specific needs of regular and distance education users, it provides integrated access to all services needed to complete the educational programmes with the following main modules:

Administrator Module

It has tools for easy creation, management and maintenance of the system. The important features of this module are:

- Approval of new study centre, region and location
- Creation of new courses
- Registration of new faculty members, department, roles, etc.
- Student online application for admission, enrolment, course allocation, promotion, etc.
- Examination schedule, announcement, forwarding of application forms, verification, issue of hall ticket
- Tracking of admission process, viewing the course content
- Report generation

Faculty Module

This module provides the framework for the faculty of any educational institution to maintain and implement the regular academic activities

- Marking and submitting student attendance, internal marks
- Daily time sheet entry of his own workload
- Tracking of online assignment and projects
- Sending and receiving feedback and comments
- Maintenance of personal schedule

- Maintenance of student diary
- Student module

This module provides the tools for the student to do the educational activities.

- Details of circular, educational events, seminar, symposium, etc.
- Weekly classroom timetable, exam schedule, etc.
- Viewing assignments and projects by the faculty
- Exam application submission
- Getting exam hall ticket
- Results announcement, dynamic provisional mark sheet
- Asynchronous collaborative learning environment between the faculty, experts
- View academic history
- Course content navigation

Content Management System

It facilitates content submission, validation, approval, retrieval, deployment and publishing of contents in digital fashion including text, images, graphics, audio, video, et in real time. It streamlines the educational content management process from content authoring, workflow, management, integration and delivery.

This interface is a systematic approach to gather, analyse, and interpret the course content for a particular course. Its main functions are as follows:

- Simplify access to quality education and training for all via multiple appropriate channels of education delivery network
- Share the knowledge base among university, learning centres, and other educational network

- Deliver the right content to the right users in a timely, scalable and cost effective manner
- Quality control
- Revision of content

Digital Library System

It provides the framework for resource collections and services, organized and categorized in support of education at all levels. It is an integrated set of services for capturing, cataloguing, storing, searching, protecting, and retrieving information and comprising digital collections, services and infrastructure to support lifelong learning, research, scholarly communication and preservation in various forms. It creates, manages, maintains a digital library as an institution and provides universal access.

Conclusion

The above article discusses all the components of an e-learning system. There may be slight variations from one system to another. But the basic components are more or less similar. It all depends upon the students and teacher to utilize all the components efficiently and effectively.

6

Web Tools in Collaborative Learning

ABSTRACT

Continuous professional development is a challenge in the education system. It is important to develop a system thorough which every individual can collaborate and support the development of each other. Teacher educators working at different levels should be linked in the collaborative manner. The potential benefits are manifold including the motivational, and knowledge enhancement aspects. In this situation, the changing trends in the use of WWW technology and web design are the panacea for the teacher educators, teachers and the students. Newer forms of web designs have emerged that aim to enhance creativity, communications, secure information sharing, collaboration, functionality of the web. The drastic developments happened in the WWW has resulted in the evolution of Web tools or Dynamic Web. There are a lot of web culture communities. Hosted services, Social-networking sites, Video sharing sites, Pod casting, mobile learning, RSS feeds are some of the new arrivals in the Dynamic Web or Semantic Web. Their applications are numerous.

Level-3 Applications are the most "Web 2.0"-oriented, exist only on the Internet. eBay, Wikipedia, and Skype are the best examples. Level-2 applications can operate offline but gain advantages from going online which benefits from its shared photo-database and from its community-generated tag database. Flickr is the best example. Level-1 applications operate offline but gain features online. Google Docs and Spreadsheets and IT uses are some examples. The Mobile devices are another technological revolution and their potentials are enormous. This paper describes some applications of the Web 2 tools in education.

Collaborative learning

With the advent of e-learning, collaborative learning is enjoying an increased share in the curricula of many schools. What we now see as individual learning will change into collaborative in future. Reasoning and intellectual development is embedded in the social situation of everyday life. So, social context of learning is important in e-learning situation.

Social Software

The term "social software" may be broadly defined as "software that supports group interaction". Although it is arguable that the Internet has always comprised a network of individuals connected through social technologies like e-mail, chat rooms and discussion boards (now referred to as the "1.0" technologies), current social software tools not only support social interaction, feedback, conversation and networking, but are also endowed with a flexibility and modularity that enables collaborative remixability—a transformative process in which the information and media organised and shared by individuals can be recombined and built on to create new forms, concepts, ideas, mashups and services.

Mejias (2005) observed that "social software can positively impact pedagogy by inculcating a desire to reconnect to the world as whole, not just the social part that exists online" (p. 1). Mejias also has a much broader definition of social software that includes the categories listed in Table 1, which encompass both Web 1.0 and 2.0 technologies. For the purposes of the current discussion, the definition adopted here, to link in with the key notion of learner control and choice, is that proposed by Dron (2007): "social software...is [where] control and structure can arise through the process of communication, not as a result of design, but as an emergent feature of group interaction" (p. 233). With this rich and varied functionality in mind, it is necessary to consider the affordances, limits and potential value adding of Web 2.0 and social software tools for learners in the Web 2.0 er.

Evolution of Web Tools

There is a drastic development in the application of web technology resulting in the development and evolution of web culture communities. Hosted services, Social-networking sites, Video sharing sites, Wikis, Blogs, Folksonomies are some to mention.

Levels of Applications

The Web 2 tools are categorized on the basis of the nature of the applications, whether they are totally dependent on the Internet or they may be used in offline also. In this way, there are three levels of applications of Web 2 tools. They are given below:

Level-3 Applications

They are the most "Web 2.0"-oriented, exist only on the Internet, deriving their effectiveness from the inter-human connections and from the network effects that Web 2.0 makes possible, and growing in effectiveness in proportion as people make more use of them. eBay, Craigslist, Wikipedia, delicious, Skype, dodgeball, AdSense are some examples to mention.

Level-2 Applications

They can operate offline but gain advantages from going online. which benefits from its shared photo-database and from its community-generated tag database? Flickr is the best example.

Level-1 Applications

Level-1 applications operate offline but gain features online. Google Docs and Spreadsheets and ITunes are some examples to mention.

Features of Web 2 websites

The characteristic features of the Web 2 tools are generally referred to as SLATES, the abbreviation of six words, Search, Links, Authoring, Tags, Extensions and Signals. Their meanings are given below:

Search

It refers to the ease of finding information through keyword search

1. **Links:** It refers to the guides to important pieces of information. The best pages are the most frequently linked to.
2. **Authoring:** The ability to constantly updating content over a platform rather than the creation of a few to being the constantly updated, interlinked work is called authoring. In wikis, the content is iterative in the sense that the people undo and redo each other's work. In blogs, content is cumulative in that posts and comments of individuals are accumulated over time.
3. **Tags:** The content developed is categorized by creating tags that are simple, one-word descriptions to facilitate searching and avoid rigid, pre-made categories.

4. **Extensions:** Automation of some of the work and pattern matching by using algorithms is referred to as extension. e.g. amazon.com recommendations.
5. **Signals:** The use of RSS (Really Simple Syndication) technology to notify users with any changes of the content by sending e-mails to them is considered as signals. This property makes the web page as dynamic web page. The web page is constantly updated and portrayed.

Wikipedia

It is a free multilingual encyclopedia project supported by the non-profit Wikimedia Foundation. Its 2 million articles (2.7 million in English) have been written collaboratively by volunteers around the world, and almost all of its articles can be edited by anyone who can access the Wikipedia website. Launched in January 2001 by Jimmy Wales and Larry Sanger it is currently the most popular general reference work on the Internet.

A wikipedia is the short name for Web Encyclopaedia. It is a collection of collaboratively authored web pages. A wiki starts with one front page. The authors can edit the page or add more pages to the wiki by creating links to new pages that don't yet exist. The content matter is edited by a team of experts. Once the content is checked for its authority, validity, and currency, that page is added to the existing content matter. It is a dynamic environment. Old versions of each page can be viewed by checking the page history. Wikis can be a powerful tool for collaborative work. The entire class can edit a document together, or the user can create group wikis which are only editable by group members.

Blogs

A *blog* is a website usually maintained by an individual with regular entries of commentary, descriptions of events, or other material such as graphics or video. Entries are commonly displayed in reverse-chronological order. Many blogs provide commentary or news on a particular subject; others function as more personal online diaries. A blog combines text, images, and links to other blogs, webpages, and other media related to its topic. The ability for readers to leave comments in an interactive format is an important part of many blogs. The word "blog" is a contraction of "web log." Blogs are a form of online journal that millions of people around the world use for self-expression and communicating with family and friends.

The author of a blog usually organizes it as a chronological series of postings. Although some groups of people contribute to blogs, there is usually only one central author for each. Blogs are growing in importance around the world. They are used by everyone from teenagers posting who they like or dislike at school to CEOs communicating directly with their customers to dissidents in oppressed populations expressing their political views. Most blogs are primarily textual, although some focus on art artlog, photographs, sketches, videos, music, audio, which are part of a wider network of social media. As of December 2007, blog search engine Technorati was tracking more than 112 million blogs. A blog is an useful tool for users. The uses of blogs are as follows:

- The user can view entries in other users' blogs. If the author prohibits this capability, the user will not be able to read any blogs on the system.
- The user can create new blog entries
- The user can edit and manage entries in her own blog or change and delete other users' entries.
- The user can create and delete user-defined tags that others may use.
- A user can create and delete the official tags that all users see.

Effective Blog Practices

Blogs are a relatively new feature, which many people are still learning how to use. There are currently very few examples of good usage of blogs. Most blogs are either blogging for the sake of blogging, or an ill-defined "learning journal" where users engage in unstructured reflection on what they are learning. It's difficult to maintain users' motivation for either of these activities. Users who are engaging in purposeful blogging for the first time will have a difficult time successfully posting without scaffolding and some clear goals due to lack of first-hand experience. Blogs give another channel to communicate with other fellow teachers and/or students. Social blogging is different from blogging in a learning environment.

You Tube

They are the video sharing website where users can upload, view and share video clips. It uses the Adobe Flash Video technology to display a wide variety of user-generated video content, including movie clips, TV clips, and music videos, as well as amateur content such as video blogging and short original videos. Most of the content uploaded by members of the public

MySpace

It is a social networking website with an interactive, user-submitted network of friends, personal profiles, blogs, groups, photos, music, and videos for teenagers and adults internationally. MySpace is the most popular social networking site. It attracts 230 000 new users per day. Bulletins boards, MySpace IM, MySpace TV, MySpace Mobile, MySpace News, MySpace Classifides, MySpace Karaoke, MySpace Polls and MySpace forums are some of the features of MySpace.

eBay

It is managed by an American Internet company named eBay.com. It is an online auction and shopping website in which people and businesses buy and sell goods and services worldwide. In addition to its original U.S. website, eBay has established localized websites in thirty other countries.

Facebook

Accounts where they can post updates of their activities to their friends. But social blogging is different from blogging in a learning environment, and you will need to work closely with your students to create effective blogs. It is recommended that you allow each student to create his own blogging goals. As David Hawkins writes in his book The Roots of Literacy, "Children can learn to read and write with commitment and quality just in proportion as they are engaged with matters of importance to them, and about which at some point they wish to read and write."

Skype

It is a software that allows users to make telephone calls over the Internet. Calls to other users of the service and to free-of-charge numbers are free, while calls to other landlines and mobile phones can be made for a fee. Additional features include instant messaging, file transfer and video conferencing. Skype-casting is a pod casting recording Skype voice over IP calls and teleconferences. The recordings would be used as podcasts allowing audio/video content over the Internet. Some of the common characteristic features of Skype are its Great Value Calls, Online number, SMS facility, Voicemail and Call forwarding, etc.

Flickr

Flickr is an image and video hosting website, web services suite, and online community platform. It was one of the earliest Web 2.0 applications. In addition to being a popular

Web site for users to share personal photographs, the service is widely used by bloggers as a photo repository. Its popularity has been fuelled by its organization tools, which allow photos to be tagged and browsed by folksonomic means. As of November 2008, it claims to host more than 3 billion images. The steps in Flickr are as follows:

- Upload
- Edit
- Organize
- Share
- Maps
- Make Stuff
- Keep in Touch

iPod

iPod is a brand of portable media players designed and marketed by Apple Inc. and launched on October 23, 2001. Over 173 million units sold worldwide as of September 2008. The general uses of iPods are iTunes Store, Games, File storage and transfer, etc. It is a good business device. It is used as a delivery mechanism for business communication and training. iPods have also gained popularity for use in education. Apple offers more information on educational uses for iPods on their website, including a collection of lesson plans.

Pod Casting

A pod cast is a series of audio or video digital media files distributed over the Internet by syndicated download, through Web feeds, to portable media players and personal computers. Though the content may be made available by direct download or streaming, a pod cast is distinguished from most other digital media formats by its ability to be syndicated, subscribed to, and downloaded automatically when new content is added. The author of a pod cast is called a pod caster. Pod casting is becoming increasingly popular in education. They enable students and teachers to share information with anyone at any time. An absent student can download the pod cast of the recorded lesson. It can be a tool for teachers or administrators to communicate curriculum, assignments and other information with parents and the community. Teachers can record book discussions, vocabulary or foreign language lessons, international pen pal letters, music performance, interviews, and debates. Pod casting can be a publishing tool for student oral presentations. Video pod casts can be used in all these ways as well.

APPLICATION OF SOCIAL SOFTWARE IN EDUCATION

General Applications

Many current social software applications straddle the virtual and real social worlds, as they entail both online and offline interactions and visual/verbal connectivity. For example, Flickr and YouTube facilitate the sharing of photos and videos within the teachers, students and other real world and virtual friends. They may form communities and collaborate in their work. Social networking sites like MySpace, Facebook and Friendster allow users to build an online identity, customize their personal profiles, interact with existing contacts and establish new relationships. Another social networking site, Stickam, additionally allows users to interact in real-time using their web cams and microphones.

Connectivity and Social Rapport

Social networking sites like MySpace, Facebook and Friendster attract and support networks of people and facilitate connections between them. They are representative of affinity spaces, where people acquire both social and communicative skills, and become engaged in the participatory culture of Web 2.0. In these spaces, users engage in informal learning, and creative, expressive forms of behaviour and identity seeking, while developing a range of digital literacies.

Collaborative Information Discovery and Sharing

Data sharing is enabled through a range of software applications, and experts and novices alike can make their work available to the rest of the online world, for example through their personal and group blogs. Social bookmarking tools such as del.icio.us, Furl and Digg allow people to build up collections of web resources or bookmarks, classify and organise them through the use of metadata tags, and share both the bookmarks and tags with others. In this way, users with similar interests can learn from one another through subscribing to the bookmarks and tags of others, and actively contribute to the ongoing growth and evolution of the "folksonomy" of web-based content and knowledge.

Content Creation

Web 2.0 emphasises the pre-eminence of content creation over content consumption. Anyone can create, assemble, organise and share content to meet their own needs and those of others. Open source and open content of Massachusetts Institute of Technology initiatives, as well as copyright licensing models like Creative Commons are helping fuel the growth of user-generated content. Wikis enable teams and individuals to work together to generate new knowledge through an open editing and review structure.

Knowledge and Information Aggregation and Content Modification

The massive uptake of Really Simple Syndication (RSS), as well as related technologies such as pod casting and vodcasting (which involve the syndication and aggregation of audio and video content, respectively, is indicative of a move to collecting material from many sources and using it for personal needs. The content can be remixed and reformulated.

Conclusion

This paper discusses various Web 2 tools available now. Till 5 years back, the Internet penetration was very low. At that time, it would be very difficult to imagine using the Web 2 tools for online collaboration. But now-a-days the Internet is easily available at many parts of the country, even at small towns and villages. It is not a problem. Many companies are providing Broadband Internet connection through cable or wireless mode. The teachers and teacher educators can use them in an efficient way for collaborative assignments. The mechanisms of interaction, communication tools and design are the major areas to be concentrated by the users. Based on these aspects and their main components, training should be given to the teachers. This will make effective online collaboration.

REFERENCES

1. Gray, D., Ryan, M. and Coulon, A. (2004). The Training of Teachers and Trainers: Innovative Practices, Skills and Competencies in the Use of eLearning. *European Journal of Open, Distance and e-Learning*. 2004 / II
2. Ham, V. and Davey, R. (2005). Our First Time: Two Higher Education Tutors Reflect on Becoming a "Virtual Teacher". Innovations in *Education and Teaching International*, 42 (3), 257-264.
3. Lam, P. and McNaught, C. (2006). Design and Evaluation of Online Courses Containing Media-enhanced Learning Materials. *Educational Media International*, 43 (3), 199–218.
4. Mason, R. (2003). Online Learning and Supporting Students. New Possibilities. In A. Tait and R. Mills (Eds.) *Re-thinking Learner Support in Distance Education: Change and Continuity in an International Context* (pp. 91-99). London: Routledge Falmer.

5. Salmon Gilly (2004). *E-moderating: The Key to Teaching and Learning Online* (2nd Edition). London: Routledge Falmer.

6. Volman, M. (2005). A Variety of Roles for a New Type of Teacher Educational Technology and the Teaching Profession. *Teaching and Teacher Education*, 21, 1 (pp. 15-31)

7. Wong, A., Quek, C.L., Divaharan,S., Liu, W.C., Peer, J. and Williams, M. (2006). Singapore Students' and Teachers' Perceptions of Computer-supported Project Work Classroom Learning Envirohments. *Journal of Research on Technology in Education*, 38 (4), 449-479.

7

Learning with Technology

The purpose of this paper is to identify key issues and questions arising from the research into new technology applications, focussing specifically on life-long learning. However, because research into new technologies tends to be sector specific, or particular to local applications and initiatives, the implications for life-long learning need to be constructed tentatively, rather than read off directly. There are also two broad literatures that currently connect hardly at all; the literature of Information and Communications Technology (ICT) and that of adult education. There is a risk that the former will dominate, given the powerful role that technology application plays in analyses of why life-long learning should be both necessary and also achievable. Indeed, as Field and Schuller have argued, some of the research now relevant to the field of life-long learning, pointedly does not engage with the adult education literature (Field and Schuller, 1999).

Research and evaluation of applications of 'new technology' in teaching and learning, has well established fields of literature and practice which now display a marked confidence. Its proponents have shown little inclination to integrate the theoretical perspectives of Duguid, Jonassen, Vygotsky and Pask with those of Freire, Knowles, Brookfield et al. As Edwards has aptly characterised it, adult education is suffering something of an identity crisis, just at the moment when its time might be seen to have arrived (Edwards, 1997, Field and Schuller, 1999).

New Technology

'New technology' is also itself a shorthand-reference to applications of communications and information technology which are changing so rapidly that the risk of generalising from what is known now, is that new applications simply by-pass current experience and render their conclusions outdated. Furthermore, the research on which this paper is based does not represent a systematic coverage of what is in use. Research and evaluation studies reflect the opportunities of available staff and funding, and are not always targeted on issues of importance for life-long learning, such as informal learning, or qualifications relevant to disadvantaged groups. There is also a 'technology lag' in terms of penetration within particular sectors and discipline areas.

The title of this paper also requires comment. 'New technology' is being used here to refer to the Internet, the World Wide Web, electronic communication and other computer based applications. We point forward to the promise of television and hand held devices for providing Web and communications functions in future. However learning opportunities which involve nothing but computer-based study are still a relatively rare phenomenon. Computer based applications are usually the most high profile element in innovative practice but they often absorb a relatively minor proportion of learner study hours, and may be used by learners as adjuncts to more familiar print, or campus based provision.

However it is the electronic delivery of information and interactive communication which is fuelling the current resurgence of life-long learning. Distance education based on print, tutor support, and perhaps limited audio and video resources, is no longer the latest technology, although it may well still be 'new technology' for many. Spokespersons for the e-University idea for example, announced that conventional distance education approaches would be likely to form the early basis for developments (THES, April 25th. 2000).

Evaluation of the outcomes of student experience with applications of computer mediated communication (CMC) and the World Wide Web have increased noticeably, in HE institutions particularly. 'Virtuality' is not yet a commonly available mode of teaching and learning. But it is here now and in use by small numbers of people, who can use their workstation to participate in real time events where learners interact on-line, from geographically dispersed locations, using streaming audio and video as well as reading words and graphics on screen.

Participation in this kind of 'new technology' is a vastly different experience from accessing CDRoms in the library of a local college. Yet both experiences might be legitimately included under the term 'New Technology'. We need to keep this breadth of experience in mind, when referring to computer based applications and also looking to the future when the television or a mobile phone might be the delivery technology.

Life-long Learning

Turning next to definitions of 'life-long learning', commentators from the adult education world in which it was launched via the Faure report of the seventies, view its current fashionability with some suspicion, as a public discourse 'narrowly confined within a short-term, economistic, new right frame' (West, 1998, p.237). Its very ubiquitousness, acclaimed by so many disparate groups, raises warning signs around its practical meaning. Its literal meaning suggests it should include the whole of education and training, from pre-school up to third age provision, and informal as well as formal and non-formal learning. Although such an approach is unmanageable for a short paper, it highlights the inter-relatedness of sectors otherwise kept separate. Improved articulation between these sectors is one of the values some proponents of lifelong learning would wish to see as a beneficial outcome.

However the research base I draw upon is not primarily focussed on sector inter-relatedness, and adopts a more conventional emphasis on adult participation in specific sectors—FE, HE, and work based learning and training. Data from the Open University is rather different in that its student body is so diverse in terms of both age, prior educational qualifications and location, that it gets closer to counting as a proxy for life-long learning. Two thirds of its students are aged between 25 and 44, 35% enter with a degree or other higher educational qualifications, roughly a third have no or low formal qualifications which would not qualify them for university entry, and the remainder have a range of A level, vocational and other awards at pre-degree level. OU students also typically cite a combination of strong work-related and personal interest goals as their main reason for study—only a minority studies for purely vocational or purely academic interest. In this way too therefore, they bring together a key issue in life-long learning—the right of adults to have access to learning opportunities which relate to their personal interests as well as to their earning capacity and the goals of their employers for more skilled employees. These points should be borne in mind where comments are made about ICT use at the OU.

Both life-long learning and ICT literatures have access and participation as key issues. However, arguments for increased provision for adults based on liberal values and achievement of human potential have never had the power (within the UK at least) to bring investment in life-long learning such as the promise of new technology is now driving.

Taking the FE sector as an example, since the Learning and Technology Committee of the FEFC (Higginson Report, 1996) recommended strategic investment across FE, both FEDA and BECTA have launched major initiatives—QUILT AND FERL—which have brought a range of changes to many FE colleges. Virtually all colleges will have a learning resources centre supporting part time study, but many now have laboratories equipped with high specification PCs, scanners, cameras, authoring tools and editing equipment and software. Halton College is one such. Newcastle College has a multimedia taster course in key skills developed jointly with Gateshead and Sunderland as part of the UfI. They also have a telematics course on use of the Internet, email and video conferencing. Waltham Forest are developing an IT based basic skills course in numeracy and literacy for local carers, as well as staff development for teachers in IT use in schools. All these colleges have been involved (with FEDA funding) in development of an evaluation tool for use with their new technology applications (Jones et at, 1999). While time pressures are so great, very little evaluation is done, and 'findings' are more often anecdotal accounts of local practice.

It is also interesting to see the boundaries between public and private sectors being reduced by projects funded out of EU ADAPT and Single Regeneration monies, both aimed at supporting retraining/training in economically threatened areas. The OU along with many other providers is using ADAPT funding to find ways of channelling provision based on its course materials, into Small and Medium Enterprises (SMEs). These developments focus on computer-based delivery methods primarily, reflecting the ICT driver in current life-long learning initiatives: '...the information-technology revolution is creating a new form of electronic, interactive education that should blossom into a life-long learning system that allows almost anyone to learn almost anything from anywhere at anytime.' (Halal and Liebowitz, 1994, quoted in Kirkup and Jones, 1995)

Computers which are in the workplace now because of the demands of IT intensive production/service methods are envisaged as delivery points for learning opportunities as well. Another interesting example of cross-sectoral investment is Connect@Sunderland, an ICT facility which aims to build links between locally based new IT intensive industries, and schools, colleges and universities in the City of Sunderland. The project includes activities such as teacher training with industrial instructors 'on the job' to make ICT relevant to both teachers and children, developing industrial links used to teach ICT with a business focus to meet national training standards, and creating a community access point bringing together industrial applications with courses provided by public sector educational institutions locally.

The co-presence of work and learning—the integration of the two—is now actively promoted by such projects and funding, not merely noticed as an interesting phenomenon for the researcher. The intention—well based or not in learning terms—is that the PC on the work desk can be used for learning needs both essential for the job, and going beyond the current job.

To conclude this section, the title of the paper yokes together two huge areas of activity and research, and we need to be aware that much more needs to be done to articulate the relationship between the two and the areas where interests are shared and those where they contrast or run counter to each other. Having made these general observations, the remainder of the paper focuses on two over-arching issues which are priority concerns in both areas—on the one hand, access and participation, and on the other, the effectiveness of learning once the barriers of 'entry' (to learning rather than to an institution necessarily) have been overcome. Accordingly, the rest of this paper is organised under these two headings, with some general comments on the research priorities which come out of the discussion of each section.

Access, Participation, Location

The promotion of new technology by UK governments via initiatives such as the National Grid for Learning and UFI'S Learn direct, is in part because of its capacity to deliver learning resources to locations readily accessible to adult learners. This issue, of the barriers confronting all adults who wish to access learning, remains a powerful concern particularly for adults in rural or disadvantaged areas. In a recent article on access issues, Watt and Paterson for example comment to the effect that 'Location of provision and flexibility of entry and exit can make or break a student's educational career' (Watt and Paterson 1999).

The comment summarises a situation in which conventional provision is perceived as making too many demands in terms of attendance for many adults to cope with, alongside work and family roles. Yet the new technology options which offer a way out of such problems via delivery to the desktop at home or work are also unlikely to be available to the typical 'access' learner from disadvantaged or low income social groups. Technology offers the solution in terms of delivery, yet the reality is that personal resources are required to a level beyond the reach of those who have typically been the target for access initiatives.

Resource Barriers Contingent on ICT Delivery of Learning

Computer ownership has risen rapidly, increasing from 26% of households in 1996-97, to 34% in 1998-99 (ONS, 29 and 30). Ownership however still reflects relative household wealth, not only because of the price of machines, but also telephone charges and space to house equipment. In 1996-97 there was also much lower access among one person households aged 60 and over. Households with children were much more likely to own a computer, with 49% of such households owning a computer in 1998-99 compared with 28% of one person households under 60. Similarly, households headed by a professional were more than four times more likely to own a computer than those headed by unskilled manual workers (ONS, 29 and 30).

The speed with which some sectors of the population have moved into use of the web emphasises the gap between those with average and above income levels, and the sharply reduced circumstances of those living below average income levels. During the 1980s there was an increase in inequality in the distribution of household disposable income, although this has slowed down since 1992. The proportion of people living in households with income below the average increased from 13% in 1961 to 21% in 1992 and fell to 18% in 1997-98 (ONS, 1999). In terms of participation in higher education, all socio-economic groups have higher rates in 1998-99 than in 1991-92 but the gap between the unskilled and professional groups has widened. Whereas unskilled participation has grown from 6% to 13%, that of Professionals has grown from 55% to 72% (ONS, 2000) . Whereas the gap was 49% it is now 59%.

Changes in the financial support for HE students have also disadvantaged those without resources other than state funding. The introduction of tuition fees in 1998-99 now means that the grant accounts for only a quarter of the support available, the rest made up by loan arrangements. The polarisation between a growing population with home or work access to computers, and a minority without any form of access, impacts on ability to acquire skills in a key area linked with employment. IT skills are highlighted as essential across semi-skilled as well as professional and skilled employment. The Open University Students Association for example is keen to support the University's use of a computer platform for various aspects of study, in part to ensure that OU students keep up with these modes of study in campus based institutions, and also gain the IT skills that employers want.

The issue of access is likely to change however, when mobile phones and hand held devices, along with television, eventually provide access to telecommunications and the Web. Mobile phone ownership has spread even more rapidly than computer ownership, with a fifth of all households in 1997-98 owning one, and two fifths of those headed by a professional. Ownership is greatest in the southeast, where three in ten households owned a mobile phone in 97-98 (ONS, 1999). BT predicts that by 2003 more people will access the Internet by phone than by personal computer (Guardian, May 9th 2000).

Educational Time Lag in ICT Application for Teaching and Learning

However, the extent to which educational providers will be able to make full use of this technology is likely to suffer a time lag such as we have seen with computer based provision, in spite of government investment, certainly in universities. Over £33million has been invested in the Teaching and Learning Technology Programme since 1992. There have been three phases of project funding, as follows:

1992-93	phase 1 – 43 projects funded
1993-98	phase 2 – 33 projects funded
1998-2001	phase 3 – 32 projects funded

Investment is focussed mainly at the level of the institution and the discipline. The current phase is attempting to learn the lessons from the first two phases, by emphasising integration with mainstream teaching, embedding ICT into teaching and learning strategies at institutional level, and continuing to promote discipline based networks and collaboration (HEFCE, 1998). A recent evaluation highlighted the limitations of what has been produced, in terms of the fact that software products are typically only designed to fit the local student population. Very little sharing or cross institutional collaboration has been initiated, although it might also be fair to say that seeking to create such a major cultural shift in periods of typically 3 to 5 years was over-ambitious.

Evaluations of TLTP and the TLTSN have shown positive outcomes in terms of increased awareness among teaching staff and a strong motivation in favour of ICT use as a means of improving the quality of students' learning. The management goal might include cost savings but teaching staff show greater awareness of the learning benefits rather than cost reduction, which in practice has not materialised. (Haywood, 1999)

Private Sector/Employment-based Access

In general, the gap between the technology rich and the technology poor has widened the disparities between adult learners. Those already employed in professional occupations are given desktop equipment which can also be used for in-house education and training as well as accredited courses enabling career development, in some cases. Those in low skilled jobs and the unemployed are deprived of such access.

Private sector providers may charge at a level which puts their provision effectively out of reach of the less well off. Provision is also likely to relate most quickly to employment related needs for those already in the more skilled end of the market. For these reasons, the learning gap between haves and have knots, is likely to linger well beyond the wide availability of home based technologies which carry educational as well as entertainment material.

Having stressed these implications for the most disadvantaged learners economically, we should note that computer based systems have played a key role in increased access and take up of provision, conventionally delivered and otherwise. An initiative like the University for Industry is only feasible because computer systems can support call centres and learner enquiries, tracking and mailing on a mass scale. Computerised administrative systems, networked resources and electronic communications, together with media based advertising, offer an essential means of increasing awareness and ensuring that potential learners make effective connection with providers. The telephone, not a 'new' technology in this context, has played a key role in breaking down the barrier of visiting a provider before the process can begin. Although UfI working now through 'Learn direct' as the brand name, will raise awareness of local provision that may or may not involve new technology, it has always been part of the aim of the initiative to increase the use of ICT as a vehicle for learning and gaining qualifications.

Special Needs

New technologies may be considered a weak strategy for recruiting more successfully from disadvantaged groups but they do offer advantages for one such group, namely those with a disability, which puts conventional provision out or reach. Home based study has always offered a key opportunity where mobility is restricted, and print plus video and audio technologies have been adapted by the Open University over 30 years of 'conventional' distance education, to suit the needs of both visual and hearing disabled learners.

The OU's 7,000 disabled students however face new barriers where web-based materials are concerned, unless providers adopt best practice in design for the disabled, and use enabling technologies as necessary. Screen magnification software for example can enable people with very poor sight to make effective use of course materials. Speech synthesisers linked to screen readers enable the blind to 'read' through listening. Vincent and Whalley describe the huge advantages that delivery of digital materials via either a CDRom or a Web site offers by contrast with audio cassette technology. These required human readers to transfer text onto tape, with university courses requiring maybe 60 or more tapes. Using the interface called ReadOut, a student can navigate, search and locate, index, bookmark and make notes about the material being communicated, and without the time consuming search and navigation procedures of the audio cassette (Vincent and Whalley, 1998 p.33).

There is also the hope that new technology might attract those alienated from education generally. There is concern for example about a minority of young men who fail at school and who do not want to return to any form of provision. In all ethnic groups, girls do as well as, or outperform boys at GCSE, and since 1998-99, girls have outperformed boys at A level. Enrolments on adult education courses include about three times as many women as men (CSO, 2000 pp 57-58). Watt and Paterson point out how little advice school leavers still get about their choices beyond school and emphasise the need for increased guidance provision for disadvantaged groups. They suggest that broadcast media already in use by these groups should be used to provide more information.

Student Support

The new technologies do also have the potential to improve access to information and guidance. Delivery over the Internet using a Web browser can bring into learners' homes an array of information about courses and student experience relevant to the enquirer's own situation and needs (Scott and Phillips, 1998). Multimedia narratives over the Web are being used at the Open University as part of services which can now be used by students in their own homes and at their own pace. Instead of a limited phone call between restricted hours, students can browse through student stories of challenges in studying and work with them and on-line 'advisers' to construct ideas for tackling them. Course choice can also be brought closer, as it were, by again providing at the desk top the kind of information about course content, prerequisites, assessment and fees which has only been available in rather complex documents or by contacting staff. Even the views of students who have studied the courses are included, and the technology does appear to add value in terms of convenience and in-depth work time by the learner.

RESEARCH ISSUES

A number of general points lead on from the discussion above:

Macro Level Monitoring of Participation Rates and Trends

It is crucial in this area of tracking participation, to have access to reliable trend data so that the impact in terms of demographic, social class and regional factors can be monitored. The current investment in life-long learning is not a guarantee of beneficial outcomes, and the analysis of its impact requires good data about the distribution of activity and outcomes.

The Census Office reports together with issue based surveys such as NIACE has sponsored, are essential for regular updates on the key question of who is participating, in what kinds of provision and to what effect. It will be interesting to see whether the UfI will publish data openly and in a form which supports researchers who want to find answers to questions about the rise and fall of participation by social class, employment, income and educational qualifications categories.

Micro Level Studies of Special Needs and Targeted Applications

In addition to the necessity of macro level studies, we should also find out how best to exploit new technologies, which offer added advantage for minority groups. Such groups include disabled learners, disaffected young men and those at risk of social exclusion. These groups are heterogeneous in their characteristics and needs, and research is needed into the design of learning opportunities which will attract each group and the diversity within them. We need to know more about how to combine the different media and technologies, and how to support effective use through support systems, which can link learners to peer groups as well as to accreditation, where these are helpful.

The Quality of the Learning Experience

The preferred modes of learning in adulthood are diverse. The learning process and its outcomes for each learner are divergent and unpredictable. In addition, prior experience and the pressures of day to day events play an influential role in whether, in what way and to what effect, learning takes place.

Into this context new technology brings possibilities we are only just beginning to exploit and evaluation provides evidence of both positive and negative effects on the quality of student learning. Before looking at some of these effects, it is worth commenting on the increased analysis of learning which has been prompted by the new possibilities technology offers and which is of value in its own right.

Designing ICT to Support Learning

Teachers now have the possibility of using a range of media and technologies and thus of deploying the particular strengths of each to their best effects. Laurillard has analysed the way in which each medium/technology supports particular aspects of the teaching/learning interaction (Laurillard, 1993). Her model of this interaction is that of a conversation or dialogue which is capable of sustaining the activities required for learning. She derives this approach from the work of Pack, among others and from a commitment to a social constructivist theory of human learning—a theory which is now dominant across the field of educational technology and ICT evaluation and development generally. It is based on the conception that the learner actively constructs meaning, and that contextual cues and supports interact powerfully with the existing frameworks and beliefs of each learner.

Laurillard's analysis of the major media forms demonstrates their capacity to support student interaction, and to provide feedback which allows students to develop their understanding. However 'telling' or moving a text might be, it is not interactive in this sense. In principle therefore, learning providers now have a much more powerful set of 'tools' in the form of multimedia and digital technologies, with which to stimulate and sustain learning.

Squires for example use the Kolb cycle to suggest how this might work (Squires, 2000). He argues that Kolb's four key stages in learning are often weakly developed. At the first stage of engagement in a practical, authentic activity, case studies and explanatory materials may be perceived as inauthentic by learners. The next stage of reflection on experience may be omitted altogether and links with the third stage of theoretical analysis are often rushed and superficial. Applying new learning in other situations at the fourth stage in the Kolb cycle is he argues, 'usually a broken link'.

ICT based materials can be designed to build in all four stages effectively, strengthening as well the links between each stage. Taking the first stage, learners are encouraged to be active explorers by even simple uses of the Web for information searching and document creation. Virtual Learning Environments go much further than this, creating 'spaces' in which learners have freedom to adjust parameters and observe the results. The TLTP materials for undergraduate geography studies, Virtual Field Course, for example, offer an open-ended environment based on maps, photographs of fieldwork sites and GIS systems designed to provide computer-based support for fieldwork and a visual environment for exploring spatially referenced information. Students can explore the physical landscape from their desktop, and thus make much better use of their time in the actual field. Post fieldwork analysis is also strengthened by further exploration of the measurements, physical features and topographical detail which the databases hold and which students can use to construct their own understanding of the field and its theories and models of the landscape.

Another example in the field of the Arts would be the Open University's Art Explorer, where students can create their own constructs for describing a number of art works available for them to view on a CDROM. Their appreciation of the specialist knowledge and language of the art critic is something they can play with and 'get inside' by being able to move around and re-size elements of well-known works which are the subject of the period under study. Other uses of technology may use simulation to provide a more limited range of possibilities for learners, but with potential just the same for learners to make better links between a personal grasp of the details of what is to be learned, and the theoretical accounts and models of the discipline.

Learners often have difficulty in 'holding together' or articulating relationships between the details of particular cases/examples/activities, and the theoretical and conceptual frameworks of a discipline. An introductory course on Object Oriented Computing at the Open University was able to improve the learning experience of its students by integrating via the onscreen medium, explanations of activities with the programming environment in use. Printed texts were given a different and complementary role with more reflective, discursive material, encouraging students to make links between their programming work and theories introduced in the course (Taylor, 1999).

The OU Science Foundation Course has also used simulations to help students come to grips with scientific models in ways which avoid complex and abstract calculation, and which do encourage people to visualise and use their imagination. A model of the way in which carbon moves through different elements and thus creates the carbon cycle is for example presented as a series of screen shots where the carbon element can be moved by the learner, feedback is provided intrinsically by questioning the learner making a false move of the carbon element, and by quiz material linked with videos which summarise and test out material taught elsewhere in the study texts provided in print.

Thus simulation, offering learners an active role in working with models not just trying to memorise them, can provide authentic learning tasks and improved understanding. Some have claimed that these approaches are more motivating because they do require the learner to be active and they do build on visual as well as other imaginations. They provide new opportunities for effective links between practical experience and theory building, when used effectively.

Moving on to Stages 2, 3 and 4 of the Kolb model, CMC and email can be used to support interactions which—given the desktop technology available and advanced design skills—can encompass a very wide range of scenarios. Reflection, theory building and practical application can all be supported drawing on a rich range of possibilities. One to one with a tutor or peer, small group discussion, moderated large conferences, role playing by learners to simulate face to face genres such as debates, buzz groups, co-counselling, seminars—all these are possible via CMC. Furthermore, real time events using technologies such as Stadium and Lyceum (http://kmi.open.ac.uk/projects/stadium/#types) can also be introduced so that learners share the same moments, whatever their geographical location or time zone. Events such as these have also been found to create added motivation and social bonding, precisely because they enforce all to be present at the same time (see Bostock, 2000 for a review of virtual learning environment functionality).

Constraints on Positive Learning Outcomes from 'New Technology'

While there are many small-scale evaluations which substantiate claims that new technology can improve the quality of learning, there are also factors which temper an overly positive view of what technology can deliver.

First, much of the computer based teaching material has been undertaken for a university context, and for recognisable and fairly stable awards within which computer mediated study might still account for a very small proportion of students' study time. A survey of institutional use of ICT in 1998 gathered evidence, which appeared to show that 40% of institutions ranked their use of ICT for teaching as low, and only 4% said that usage was high. By contrast, 54% of institutions ranked their use for research purposes as high, and 37% their use for administration purposes as high also. The impact of TLTP materials is high in those disciplines where computing is essential to the research base—archaeology, veterinary science, biosciences, economics, and so on, but low in others where it is not (Haywood et al, 1999). Many students are thus still likely to spend most of their study time reading books, attending seminars and lectures and producing written papers.

We also lack evidence of the effectiveness of new technology for support of learning outcomes for pre-degree and vocational qualifications, in institutions other than universities and in the workplace. The OU's Learning Support for Small Businesses Project, in collaboration with the Universities of Central England and Wolverhampton and with the Birmingham City Council, aims to deliver training and business support via the Internet, to SMEs in the West Midlands. However achieving the goals of such projects is difficult. Employers want their workers to access only the immediately necessary, and in the shortest possible time. Providers find it difficult to match exactly the diversity of these needs, or provide just what is wanted, whenever it is wanted. While new technology can in theory achieve workplace learning which is 'just in time and just enough', the reality is still some way off.

Second, life-long learning is displaceable learning - it so often has to give way to demands for time from other areas. To take evidence from just one context, but in relation to thousands of adult learners, year on year, OU students who drop out from study, are surveyed and around a third respond that it is pressures from their work and family context that are the reason. About one fifth also say that they underestimated the time required for study. Qualitative studies have in addition shown how prior educational and learning experience can influence the likelihood of further study either positively or negatively, depending on the quality of that prior learning.

Furthermore, we may be open to the use of different media ourselves, but so time short that we can only take a 'satisfying' approach to learning. We have no time to do more than skim and sketch in the meanings of what we are learning and cannot give time to explore resources, check out conferences or bulletin boards for new understandings. Indeed, if anything could be a safe generalisation for adult learners below retirement age, (and for many, beyond it), 'time challenged' would apply to most. Where the effort of using new technology lengthens access to information or awareness, such learners will vote with their feet. We have evidence in an OU context for example that courses which use the computer as an essential requirement, whether for conferencing, delivery or CD-ROM access, typically require more time for study, if only because the set up and use of hardware and software is an add-on to the content of the course. We have also found that workplace learners do not necessarily want to use their computer for learning even where home access and personal skills are not at issue. One large employer engineered use of the same communications environment for OU study as for communication at work. Students hardly used it in part because they had had enough of interaction with their screens at work, and felt that their course units provided as much as they needed—or wanted—in order to get their MBA.

Cultural Factors

While new technology offers immensely powerful tools through which understanding can be initiated, scaffold and resourced, our existing culture and circumstances as learners can erect barriers. Some of our preferences for or against particular media for example, reflect the impact of existing learning cultures, notably the assumption that what the greatest authority is in 'black and white' carries. Some learners are also highly instrumental, rejecting the possibility of deepening their learning if that requires additional time 'on task' using the media rich resources of a multimedia package. If the core texts are located in print materials, for these learners it is the print materials they will choose, whether or not these work as effectively for them or not.

Finally, issues of personal identity, self image and power come into play. Some learners welcome computer based study precisely because they do not have to interact with a teacher. The computer can deliver messages stripped of their power to embarrass or to remind the learner of their negative experiences in the past. Computer marked tests and computer based feedback offer preferred modes for some learners, whether because of release from negative aspects of their own identity or their past experiences of interactions around learning.

In the context of CMC, it has also been found that some learners communicate more easily at a distance because they are not intimidated by the impressions created by others in the group, or the dominance of a tutor (Mason, 1994, Joinson, 1998). Brookfield has commented on the strong preference adult educators have for the face to face circle of learners as the ideal, democratic 'theatre' for equality in interaction. He warns against this view, pointing out that the under confident can feel oppressed by this format, required to speak rather than freed by their position of apparent equality. 'The circle can be experienced as mandated disclosure, just as much as it can be a chance for people to speak in an authentic voice' (Brookfield, 1998, p 140). Brookfield has begun to give his students permission to be silent if that is their wish, offering an explicit 'no-speech policy' as a way of creating a more positive inner freedom than the circle actually delivers.

It is interesting that experienced moderators of CMC are also recognising that the pejorative term for those who read but do not post messages, 'lurkers', fails to do justice to the nature of participation online, and the feelings that accompany participating. There are many recorded instances of learners who feel intimidated by the apparent expertise of those who do participate, and fearful of reactions to their own messages. Some learners therefore do not find CMC a liberating experience, and need much longer than average to become accustomed to the undermining effects of loss of familiar cues and conventions (see Feenberg 1989 for an excellent analysis of the decontextualising effects of CMC).

On the other hand, some learners feel released from aspects of their own identity and able to create an on-line identity which they may feel is in some ways different from their face to face interactions. Technology enables such post modern identity shifts, and there may be potential here for recreating confidence or more coherent identities, in lives which have been threatened by challenges to personal identity and stability, such as unemployment, or relationship loss may create (West, 1998, p 238).

Some forms of identity freedom have manifested themselves in disinherited behaviour which can create stress for others, as in instances where 'flaming' occurs. Joinson has also explored the role of self awareness and visual anonymity, as helping explain the increased self-disclosure which has been noticed in CMC behaviour (Joinson, 1999). Research into use of the Internet is revealing how online behaviour manifests itself in ways which carry quite different outcomes for different people and their social networks. Some do reveal more of themselves and enter into new relationships online which may be more intense than those they have with old friends. Others may spend so much time online that their existing family and friendship circles suffer. Wallace quotes this rather apocalyptic vision of Stoll's, of the Internet as a negative force: 'It's an unreal universe, a soluble tissue of nothingness. While the Internet beckons brightly, seductively flashing an icon of knowledge-as-power, this non-place lures us to surrender our time on earth. A poor substitute it is, this virtual reality where frustration is legion and where—in the holy names of Education and progress—important aspects of human interactions are relentlessly devalued.' (Stoll, 1995, quoted in Wallace, 1999, p.233)

Educators who have developed CMC learning environments have noticed from the beginning a small proportion of users who 'get hooked' and spend far more time online than the programme designers intended or felt was necessary to achieve the desired ends. 'The Internet as a time sink' is a telling phrase for the way in which, for all of us, this new technology sometimes has inefficiencies in information provision and communication, which make it more time consuming for simple transactions than old technologies such as the telephone (Wallace, 1999).

RESEARCH ISSUES

The scale of the task facing research here is enormous, given the early stage in our use of new technology. My suggestions are but a starting point, and reflect my own particular interests in the life-long learning field. I have made suggestions in two areas: sub-degree and vocational learning, and genres/prototype development.

Vocational and Sub-degree Strategies

Inspite of the QUILT and FERL initiatives, we lack effective evaluations of how to use new technology to deliver the kinds of learning which the focus is for FE and workplace training. So much of the development work and evaluation has been done in HE, that we have little evidence for how to use the technology effectively outside this context. In the early eighties when Open and Distance Learning was taken up by industry and employers, the need for evaluation was shrugged off in the idea that 'they keep on buying the package so it must work'. This cannot be an effective approach where new technologies are concerned, and we must find ways of funding qualitative evaluations of technology in use for learning associated with vocational and sub-degree level study.

Genre Studies and Adaptable Prototypes

CMC has generated an enormous literature because it uses off the shelf software such as First Class, WebCT etc, which providers can use relatively easily to encourage communication with and between their learners. What this literature shows us is how much richer and more subtle are the interactions we can create when we structure our environment and bring small groups of independent learners together, with the confidence to create their own knowledge (Musselbrook et al, 2000, Haughey and Anderson, 1998, Burge and Roberts, 1998) We have already learned enough for many to assert that this is a new medium, and that the skills of effective facilitation face to face are different and do not necessarily transfer. Computer mediated communication is but one 'genre' of new technology, and we are already aware of the diversity of ways in which it can be deployed.

We need a similar concentration upon other genres, to provide models for good practice and robust strategies, which have been proven across multiple usages and contexts. When the new applications are taken up for teaching and learning purposes, we need to evaluate and share our learning about what works, with whom, for what and in what circumstances.

Some Key Research Question Here

How can designers/teachers provide the most effective trade-off for learners, between richness and complexity of the media/technologies used, against the 'pay off' in terms of learning outcomes and economy of time on task for the learner?

How can learning providers ensure that evaluation is built-in and routine, and influences future course/materials design?

How are minority learner needs best catered for, their interests built into design considerations along with the majority?

How can we ensure that the diversity between learners in terms of their skills in using different media and technologies (including TV as well as the computer and hand held devices), is properly supported through the design of ICT based learning environments?

How can we avoid media colonisation and media imperialism, whereby one medium, such as the Web, takes over roles more properly performed via other media, or soaks up investment in materials creation, to the detriment of other, cheaper media or media more accessible or effective for particular sub groups?

How can we build learning communities which encourage active critical learners, and which build learner skills in learning across diverse environments and media models?

Should we/can we avoid the promotion of learning as a lifestyle choice—ICT can blur the boundary between consumerism and learning?

Concluding Thoughts on Institutional Change

The purpose of this paper has been to open up issues not to come to conclusions. However it would be misleading not to mention the impact on public sector institutions for education and training which is being generated by the synergies between new technologies and life-long learning. Edwards and Usher have drawn attention to the displacement of education by the discourse of lifelong learning and learners, dissolving the boundaries round education as a distinctive activity, 'invested with the missionary project of the educator' (Edwards and Usher, 1998, p.100). There is a growing integration between learning and commerce, which has markedly accelerated with the arrival of technologies that enable intensive communication and interaction at a distance. The pages of the Times Higher provide ever new examples of partnerships between public sector education institutions the world over, and corporations from the worlds of publishing, telecommunications and broadcasting, who are linking up in order to sell content to business as well as individuals.

The latest at the time of writing is a double spread coverage which takes in the World Education Market in Vancouver, the African Virtual University, Universities 21 and its negotiations with News Corporation to form a joint venture company (THES, May 19th 2000). With the exception of AVU which is World Bank sponsored, the language is also straight from commerce—intellectual property, the brand name, revenue stream and so on. The quoted comments of the vice-chancellor of Melbourne, chairman of Universities 21 assert that 'e-education is the way to go'. Neither individual campus 'brands' nor 'old-fashioned forms of pedagogy and their adaptation (sic) to distance education' are the way ahead. Instead, the global market requires a global brand and custom designed e-education programmes. It is hardly surprising to find on the same page that Canada's Council of Ministers of Education are concerned to prevent their country's public education curriculum from being effectively dominated by commercial suppliers of materials.

Whatever the chances of the Canadian ministers, they will not be able to put the genie back into the bottle, and none of our public sector institutions face anything other than continual change, and in some cases collapse or mutation into a radically different kinds of organisation. Barnett has called this an age of super complexity (Barnet, 2000), but it is also an age which requires good strategies for institutional survival. The impact on research of this flux and uncertainty is likely to be mixed. Some of the issues raised require long-term commitment to essential data collection and monitoring of change. They also suggest that sectors which have not traditionally been effectively resourced to do evaluation let alone research—FE notably—require such resource if we are to use new technologies effectively. As Mayes has emphasised, greater insight into pedagogic innovation may be gained through 'focussing on the social dimension of communities of learners' and thus we cannot afford to ignore learning contexts and the effects upon them of institutional change and discontinuity (Mayes, 2000).

There may be little chance of taking up the research challenges we currently face, unless we are prepared to assert the need for resources channelled to key areas. It is undoubtedly a period of 'interesting times' and one in which life-long learning is also creating new research opportunities and attracting new interest. We shall need shared values to help drive collaboration, and these might be found through constructing research agendas such as the present exercise of the colloquium.

REFERENCES

1. Barnett, R. (2000) *Realizing the University in an Age of Super Complexity*, Buckingham: Society for Research into Higher Education and Open University Press.
2. Bostock, S. (2000) Virtual Learning Environments in Educational Developments, issue 1.1, 17-18.
3. Brookfield, S.(1998) Against Naive Romanticism: From Celebration to the Critical Analysis of Experience, Studies in Continuing Education, Vol. 20, No. 2, pp. 127-42.
4. Burge, L. and Roberts, J.M. (1998) Classrooms with a Difference: Facilitating Learning on the Information Highway, Montreal: Cheneliere/McGraw-Hill.
5. Edwards, R. (1997) Changing Places? Flexibility, Life-long Learning and a Learning Society, London: Routledge.
6. Edwards, R. and Usher, R. (1998) Lo(o)s(en)ing the Boundaries: from "Education" to "Life-long Learning", Studies in Continuing Education, Vol. 20, No. 1, pp. 83-103

7. Feenberg, A. (1989) The Written World, in Mason, R. and Kaye, A. (eds) *Mindweave,* Oxford: Pergamon, pp. 22-39.

8. Field J. and Schuller, T. (1999) Investigating the Learning Society, Studies in the Education of Adults, Vol. 31, No. 1, pp. 1 - 9.

9. Haywood, J. Anderson, C., Day, K. Land, R. and Macleod, H. (1999) Use of TLTP Materials in UK Higher Education, Edinburgh, Centre for Teaching, Learning and Assessment, Department of Higher and Further Education.

10. Haughey, M. and Anderson, T.(1998) Networked Learning: The Pedagogy of the Internet, Montreal: Cheneliere/McGraw-Hill.

11. HEFCE, September 1998/47 Review of CTI and TLTSN: An Evaluation of the Computers in Teaching Initiative and Teaching and Learning Technology Support Network, Bristol: Higher Education Funding Council for England.

12. Joinson, A. (1998) Causes and Implications of Disinhibited Behaviour on the Internet, in XXX Psychology and the Internet: Intrapersonal, Interpersonal, and Transpersonal Implications.

13. Joinson, A. (1999) Self-disclosure in Computer-mediated Communication: The Role of Self-awareness and Visual Anonymity, Milton Keynes: Institute of Educational Technology, Open University, Mimeo.

14. Jones, A. Barnard, J. Thompson, J. Calder, J. and Scanlon, E. (1999) Learning with IT; Final Report RPM 050, Milton Keynes: The Open University, Institute of Educational Technology.

15. Kirkup, G. and Jones, A. (1995) New Technologies for Open Learning: The Superhighway to the Learning Society, in Raggatt, P., Edwards, R. and Small, N. (eds) The Learning Society: Challenges and Trends, London: Routledge, pp. 272 -292.

16. Laurillard, D. (1993) Rethinking University Teaching: A Framework for the Effective Use of Educational Technology, London: Routledge

17. Mason, R. (1994) Using Communications Media in Open and Flexible Learning, London: Kogan Page

18. Mayes, T. (2000) Pedagogy, Life-long Learning and ICT, Centre for Research in Life-long Learning, Gasgow Caledonian University (Mimeo)

19. Musselbrook, K., McAteer, E. Crook, C. Macleod, H. Tolmie, A. (2000) Learning Networks and Communications Skills, Association for Learning Technology Journal, Vol. 8, No. 1 71 – 79

20. Office for National Statistics, (1999) Social Trends 29 Office for National Statistics, (2000) Social Trends 30, Her Majesty's Stationery Office, London.
21. Scott, P. and Phillips, M. (1998) Developing Web-based Student Support Systems: Telling Student Stories on the Internet, in Vincent, T. and Eisenstadt, M. (eds) The Knowledge Web: Learning and Collaborating on the Net, London:Kogan Page.
22. Squires, D. (2000) The Impact of ICT Use on the Role of the Learner, Life-long Learning in Europe, Vol. V, Issue 1, pp. 55-61.
23. Stoll, C. (1995) *Silicon Snake Oil*, New York: Anchor Books
24. Taylor, J. and Tosunoglu, C. (1999) M206 Evaluation Report 1998, Programme on Learner Use of Media, Paper No. 122, Milton Keynes: The Open University, Institute of Educational Technology
25. Vincent, T. and Whalley, P. (1998) The Web: Enabler or Disabler, in Vincent, T. and Eisenstadt, M. (eds) The Knowledge Web: Learning and Collaborating on the Net, London:Kogan Page
26. Wallace, P.M. (1999 *The Psychology of the Internet*, Cambridge: Cambridge University Press
27. Watt, S. and Paterson, L.C. (2000) Pathways and Partnerships: Widening Access to Higher Education, Journal of Further and Higher Education, Vol. 24, No. 2, pp. 107-116.
28. West, L. (1998) The Edge of a New Story ? On Paradox, Post-modernism and the Cultural Psychology of Experiential Learning, Studies in Continuing Education, Vol. 20, No. 2, pp. 235-249.

8

Cross Border Education

ABSTRACT

In the last few years, internationalization and globalization of higher education has been a well discussed issue amongst scholars and practitioners in the field of higher education. The effects of globalization of education has brought rapid developments in learning systems across the world in social, economic, political, and technological fields. Due to the increased demand for education and the recent developments in the Information and Communication Technologies (ICT) has accelerated the growth of cross border education. A number of agencies and educational institutions have started exploring the possibilities of providing education across national boundaries and in most cases technology supported education. General Agreement in Trade and Services has greatly influenced the process of education in the recent past. As per GATS the educational services can be divided into 4 major categories in 5 major sectors. Nowadays education is no more considered as a free service, but as a commodity which can be traded between corporate companies and countries as well.

Nowadays education can be owned, bought, sold, transferred, leased, and so on and so forth. There are many apprehensions and fears among the political leaders, academicians, and industrialists about the impact of globalization on the marginalized countries and people as well. But so far there are few studies had been conducted to find out the perceptions of the major stake holders, i.e., students about the effect of cross border education. This study was taken to find out the main issues considered important by the student teachers and their perceptions about these issues. Economic, Educational, Socio-cultural, Technological, Linguistic, Political, Age, Gender, Geographical, Historical, Ethnic, Philosophical, Biological are some of the dimensions of Cross Border Education. The Educational, Socio-cultural, Economic and Technological dimensions of Cross Border Education are considered as the most important by the study and the students' perceptions have been found out.

Introduction

In the last few years, internationalization and globalization of higher education has been a well discussed issue amongst scholars and practitioners in the field of higher education. The effects of globalization on education bring rapid developments in learning systems across the world as ideas, values and knowledge, changing the roles of students and teachers, and producing a shift in society from industrialization towards an information-based society. Communication and information technologies represented by the Internet made the provision of higher education services across national borders possible. There have been changes in the labor market, which have resulted in calls for more knowledge and skilled workers, and workers with deeper understandings of languages, cultures and business methods all over the world. In today's environment, education provides individuals with a better chance of employment, which in turn leads to a better lifestyle, power and status. The commoditization of knowledge as intellectual property causes tensions between the more profitable applied subjects of science and technology, and those of basic theoretical enquiry, particularly in arts and humanities. It also creates institutional winners and losers. The entry of the institutions from the developed western countries into the developing countries had resulted mixed responses. Some believe that this process is an invaluable opportunity for the people of the developing countries to raise their skills and standards of education. Others fear that it is merely a modern version of cultural imperialism that will lead to the creation of a Western society.

WTO/GATS Specifications

The rise of a global society, driven by technology and communication developments is shaping children, the future citizens of the world into 'global citizens', intelligent people with a broad range of skills and knowledge to apply to a competitive, information based society. Education is becoming a life-long learning and training process developing transferable skills and knowledge that can be applied to competitive markets where knowledge and information is being traded as a commodity. The current WTO/GATS negotiations also facilitate globalization of higher education markets. The formalization process of trade liberalization through the WTO and its overarching General Agreement on Trade in Services (GATS) have introduced trade in education with several new dimensions attached to it, which were hitherto unknown to the world of education especially in the developing countries. In the framework of the WTO/GATS negotiations, four modes of trading services are defined. They are described as given in Table 8.1.

Table 8.1. Various modes of trading as specified by GATS

Mode	Definition	Examples	Potential
Cross Border Supply	Service crosses the border and the consumer does not move	ODL e-Learning Virtual Universities	Great
Consumption Abroad	Consumer moves to the country of the supplier	Studying abroad	High
Commercial Presence	Service provider establishes his presence in other country	Franchise Twinning	Growing
Presence of Natural Persons	Movement of Professionals	Professors, teachers working abroad	Moderate

At present, the second category i.e., studying abroad is the normal trend. But, nowadays, with the advances in the ICT, it is common to see the online courses everywhere and the Universities are also establishing their presence in other countries through collaboration and franchising, twinning, etc. This is slowly gaining momentum and the future is very strong for ICT based learning. GATS have specified the services into many categories. They are given as per Table 8.2.

Table 8.2. Classification of Education services under GATS

Category of Education Services	Education Activity
Primary Education CPC 921	Pre-school and other primary educational services
Secondary Education CPC 922	Higher secondaryTechnical and Vocational Secondary
Higher Education CPC 923	Other post secondary education, graduation
Adult Education CPC 924	Education for adults
Other Education CPC 929	Covers all other education services

Most of the foreign institutions are vying for the market in higher education. There is very negligible presence in the Secondary and Primary sectors. This may lead to educational imbalances among the countries.

VARIOUS DIMENSIONS OF CROSS BORDER EDUCATION

Socio-economic Dimension

The Globalization has altered the map of the whole world and has had its associated impact on the social sector. It has made significant impact in the economic, social, political and cultural aspects as well. On the one hand there is growing affluence and on the other hand there is greater deprivation. The challenge ahead is to foster the many learning opportunities to the most marginalized ones like women, poor, living in rural areas, the socially backward people, etc. There are on one side, breathtaking advances in Science and Technology, and on the other side, there is massive poverty, socio-economic inequality and political marginalization. Out of the 800 million illiterate adults worldwide, 70% are from Sub-Saharan Africa and East and South Asia. Girls account for about 57% of out of school primary school age children and 60% of them are from Arab States and South and West Asia. To address the crisis the countries met at the United Nations in 2000 and signed the Millennium Declaration containing time bound development targets better known as Millennium Development Goals to be achieved by 2015. They are :

1. Eradication of Extreme Poverty
2. Achieving Universal Primary Education
3. Reducing Child Mortality
4. Promoting Gender Equity
5. Improving Maternal Health
6. Combating AIDS/HIV/... etc.

7. Ensuring sustainable development
8. Developing global partnership for development.

Of the eight MDGs, three are education related and the five others require inputs from the education sector. It is the primary duty of all the countries to achieve this goal. The same sentiment was echoed in the Minister of HRD, GOI, Shri. Arjun Singh during his speech at the 2nd Mega University Summit – GMUNET organized by IGNOU. In this backdrop, we should know the role of Cross Border Education in achieving these goals because it is the primary role of the state to look after the education of all the people.

Technological Dimension

Information and Communication Technologies have created global connectivity at the same time created a widening gap between the information rich and information deprived. As far as India is concerned, there is a need for networking and sharing of resources for keeping the costs within reasonable limits, for making the technology accessible to the grassroot learners. The other technological issues are related to the integrating media, convergence of various technologies, and the proper and full utilization of the powers of ICT for the development of the marginalized people. Already there is a feeling that the ICTs have created a digital divide. There are wide variations between the technology affluent countries and those at the margin. The Internet users in U.S. are 551 per 1000, whereas in India it is only 16 and in Bangladesh, it is 2.

The developed nations have more access to Telephone, Internet, Mobile phone etc and have higher literacy rates, per capita income and they spend more % of their GDP on education. The situation is brim in the developing and underdeveloped countries. How to reduce the digital divide, so that everybody may access education? This is a big question to be answered. Developing countries like Africa, highly populated South Asian countries like India, Pakistan and Bangladesh are the most likely targets for international collaborative efforts for the dissemination of education. This is basically due to the surge in demand for educational products in this part of the world and the consequent high financial returns for the provision of these products.

Educational Dimension

In the educational front, there is a stir among the academic community over many issues. Reduction in the autonomy of the academia and researchers, the changing of educational institutions into corporate style of functioning, increasing cost of education, the access, equity, local institutions losing their uniqueness, westernization, and the superiority of English over other languages, etc are some of the current issues being debated among the academic circles. They must be resolved first before taking any initiative to cross border education and signing the GATS.

The Need for this Study

In India, the term cross border education globalization has been hotly debated over a decade. But the main people involved are mostly the industrialists, academic administrators, media, politicians and bureaucrats. There are very few ground level studies related to the thoughts and perceptions of the grassroot persons, i.e., students of both higher education and at secondary level. So, this study was taken up by the author to find out what are the issues the student teachers think important related to globalization and their perceptions this regard.

Sample

250 student teachers took part in this study. The sampling was made on a voluntary basis. They were from various economic

backgrounds, rural or urban surroundings, educational qualifications, and age. Their average age is 24.91. In all categories, the number of participants is almost equal.

Methodology

As there is no testing instrument readily available, it was decided to make one such instrument with the help of the participants and then to test it on them. This experiment is done in two phases. The first phase was to find out the major issues related to cross border education and their relative importance perceived by the participants. During the second phase, the final testing instrument was prepared and administered to the participants and the final results were presented.

PHASE I—A: IDENTIFICATION OF THE MAJOR ISSUES AND THEIR RELATIVE IMPORTANCE

In the first phase the Brainstorming technique was used to elicit various issues related to the impact of cross border education and the relative importance given to them by the participants. The participants were asked to write as many issues as possible and write them on the given sheet of paper within the given time. Once it was over, the papers were collected and analyzed for the main issues and how many participants have mentioned them in their response. Items which were similar in meaning and nature but mentioned by different names by the participants were given a common name suitable to the items. Some experts were called to identify the items and put them in different category to avoid any subjectivity. The following table lists various items and the number of participants who had mentioned them as the possible important issue related to globalization. This method was used to elicit maximum number of issues and their relative importance as perceived by the participants in a natural and free way.

Table 8.3. The issues related to cross border education and their relative importance as perceived by the participants

S.No.	Issue	Number of participants mentioned
01.	Economic	170
02.	Educational	167
03.	Socio-cultural	165
04.	Technological	157
05.	Linguistic	118
06.	Political	116
07.	Age	113
08.	Gender	109
09.	Geographical	107
10.	Historical	105
11.	Ethnic	114
12.	Philosophical	93
13.	Biological	46

From the table it is clear that as many as 13 issues were mentioned by the participants varying from economic to biological ones. Their relative importance felt by the students are also given. It is understood by the table that the Economic, Technological, Socio-cultural and Educational issues are the most important ones. So, it was decided that the items which were mentioned by more than half of the participants would be selected for further analysis. As per this criterion, the items for further discussion in this study are:

1. Economic
2. Educational
3. Socio-cultural
4. Technological

PHASE I—B : THE IDENTIFICATION OF THE ITEMS IN EACH MAJOR ISSUE

In this phase also the same brainstorming method was used to elicit as many items as possible in each major issue identified by the participants. The participants were asked to write as many points in each issue as they deem fit. By the same methodology applied in the Phase I, similar items were clubbed together and the wordings were reframed without affecting the original meaning so as to fit into the final questionnaire. The items were of Likert type Scale ranging from 1 = Fully disagree, 2 = Disagree, 3 = Neutral, 4 = Agree, 5 = Fully agree. Items were framed both in the positive and negative type so as to avoid monotonous marking. In this way the final questionnaire was prepared which is presented in the following sections.

PHASE—II : PARTICIPANTS' PERCEPTIONS RELATED TO THE IMPACT OF GLOBALIZATION

In this phase, the final questionnaire was prepared and all the statistical prerequisites such as reliability, validity, item analysis, discrimination etc were scrupulously followed. It was administered among the participants and the final result is presented issue wise. The count for each item by each participant was entered in MS Excel Spreadsheet and SPSS 11.5 version was used for the statistical analysis throughout this experiment. In every perception rating, the trend analysis technique is used. This will tell whether the issue is considered important or not by most of the participants.

RESULTS

Economic Issues

This section consists of 13 items which were chosen by the participants. The following table presents the items and their mean score, the standard deviation and the trend analysis. The items with mean more than 3 are given an upward arrow mark and below 3 are represented by a downward arrow. The same trend is applicable to all the further categories.

Table 8.4. The Mean and S.D. of the Items in the Economic Issues

S.No.	Item	Mean	S.D.	Trend
01.	Cross Border Education has introduced market driven competition among unequal partners	4.434	1.257	▲
02.	Cross Border Education causes a shift from supply driven economy into a demand driven economy	4.417	0.895	▲
03.	Cross Border Education leads to the privatization of education	3.342	1.794	▲
04.	Cross Border Education leads to the self financed educational programmes	3.318	2.925	▲
05.	Cross Border Education leads to the economic supremacy of the industrialized countries	4.573	1.896	▲
06.	Cross Border Education leads the Institutions to self sustain themselves	3.275	2.012	▲
07.	Education may be treated as a commodity which can be owned, purchased or sold.	1.769	0.869	▼
08.	Cross Border Education will maintain the need of the economically marginalized people.	2.908	1.021	▼
09.	Cross Border Education will increase the divide between the rich and the poor	4.553	0.873	▲

S.No.	Item	Mean	S.D.	Trend
10.	Cross Border Education will minimize the cost of education	1.698	0.842	▼
11.	Cross Border Education will strengthen the links between the Indian labour market and education	1.586	0.673	▼
12.	The security of the institutions will be preserved by Cross Border Education	2.857	1.247	▼
13.	Cross Border Education leads to the two way mobilization of resources	2.861	0.769	▼

As Table-8.4 shows, the results are mixed. For most of the items, the mean values are ranging above 3 which shows that most of the participants have perceived education cannot be treated as a commodity as specified by GATS. For some questions related to the self financing and privatization, the mean values are ranging just above 3 which mean that the participants are not sure about it. This table shows that the student teachers are still in the traditional Indian mindset that Education is a service, not a commodity. And still it appears that student teachers have some apprehensions about the supremacy of the western countries over the developed countries.

Educational Issues

This section consists of 12 items which were chosen by the participants. The following table 8.5 presents the items and their mean score and the standard deviation.

As Table 8.5 shows, for most of the items, the mean values range between 2 and 3, which means that the participants are not fully in flavour of the Cross Border Education as far as the educational matters are concerned. For the items related to the autonomy of education and research, most

Table 8.5. The Mean and S.D. of the items in the Educational Issues

S.No.	Item	Mean	S.D.	Trend
01.	The Cross Border Education will lead to the improvement in quality education	3.107	1.731	▲
02.	Dissemination of knowledge will be enhanced by Cross Border Education	3.253	1.652	▲
03.	Cross Border Education will support the creation of knowledge	2.783	0.989	▼
04.	Cross Border Education contribute to the maintenance of the uniqueness of the institutions	2.342	1.894	▼
05.	Cross Border Education will maintain the autonomy and control of the teachers over their work	1.864	0.856	▼
06.	Cross Border Education will maintain the autonomy and control of the researchers.	1.750	0.843	▼
07.	Cross Border Education will reduce the power of the learners.	2.764	1.587	▼
08.	Cross Border Education will result in the improvement of the literacy level	1.795	1.218	▼
09.	Cross Border Education will lead to the repackaging of available course materials	3.869	0.249	▲
10.	Cross Border Education will lead to the collaboration of institutions	3.842	1.543	▲
11.	Cross Border Education leads the educational institutions to function in a corporate style	4.217	1.265	▲
12.	Cross Border Education will lead to the immediate and long-term knowledge based curriculum	3.082	1.746	▲

participants opined that it may affect the autonomy. Most of the participants have the idea that the institutions will function like corporate entities.

Socio-cultural Issues

This section consists of only 9 items which were chosen by the participants. The following table presents the items and their mean score and the standard deviation.

Table 8.6. The Mean and S.D. of the items in the Socio-Cultural Issues

S.No.	Item	Mean	S.D.	Trend
01.	Cross Border Education will enhance the service to the community	1.884	1.359	▼
02.	It is disadvantageous to the developing countries	3.681	0.584	▲
03.	Cross Border Education will maintain the need of the socially marginalized people.	2.165	0.862	▼
04.	Cross Border Education will increase the access of education to all the people	1.113	0.462	▼
05.	Cross Border Education will eliminate the cultural focus and educational themes	3.148	1.575	▲
06.	Cross Border Education will lead to the Westernization	2.367	1.105	▼
07.	English will dominate the Cross Border Education process	4.546	1.259	▲
08.	Cross Border Education will preserve the linguistic values	2.273	1.657	▼
09.	Cross Border Education will preserve the moral and ethical values of the individual communities	3.176	1.250	▲

As Table 8.6 shows, in this issue also the results are mixed. The value 1.113 for item 4 and 1.884 for item 1 show that very few people have the belief that Cross Border Education will serve the community and increase the access to all the people. There is widespread belief that the Cross Border Education process is reserved only for rich, urban, English speaking literati. As seen throughout the world, English is ruling the roost. Still in India, English is highly preferred in comparison with local languages. This survey confirms these facts.

Technological Issues

This section consists of only 6 items which were chosen by the participants. The following table presents the items and their mean score and the standard deviation.

Table 8.7. The Mean and S.D. of the items in the Technological Issues

S.No.	Item	Mean	S.D.	Trend
01.	The Cross Border Education will serve the interests of the countries which have already attained higher level of technology	4.122	1.135	▲
02.	ICT has the potential vehicle for Cross Border Education	4.785	0.984	▲
03.	ICT has the potential for commoditizing the education function	4.236	1.158	▲
04.	ICT has the potential for commoditizing the research function	4.132	1.102	▲
05.	ICT will transform the present campus education into virtual education	4.751	0.867	▲
06.	Cross Border Education will drive the quick adoption of ICT	3.769	1.386	▲

From Table 8.7 it is seen that for most of the items, the mean values are above 3.5. It shows the strong feeling among the student teachers about the powers of ICT. It is a well proved and well expected result throughout the world. Once again in this experiment it is reconfirmed.

Discussion

The results of this experiment clearly found out issues which the student teachers feel important as far as Cross Border Education is concerned, and the perceptions about these issues. The responses are mixed in nature. On some issues the participants have a positive opinion, whereas on many of the issues, they do not have positive opinion. India being deep rooted in its cultural religious and social setup, the participants may think that the Cross Border Education may disturb them. The results of this study cannot be taken as final, as some other issues are not taken for consideration, and the sample size is relatively small. Further extensive studies are needed in this direction, so that the clear picture may evolve.

REFERENCES

1. Arjun Singh: (2005). Inaugural Address at the ICDE International Conference on Open Learning and Distance Education. Nov. 19-23. IGNOU, New Delhi.
2. Balakrishnan, N. (2002). *Information and Communication Technologies and the Digital Divide in the Third World Countries.* Cultural Science, 81 (8), 966-972.
3. GATS *"General Agreement on Trade in Services"* Website:www.wto.org/english/tratop_e/serv_e/gatsqa_e.html
4. Gill, S.S. (2003). *Cross Border Education: Higher Education will Suffer*. *The Tribune*, July 20, 2003.
5. GOI (2001-2002). *Selected Education Statistics*. New Delhi. Department of Education.
6. Khan, A.W. (2003). *Shaping the Future with Knowledge: Empowerment Through Education and Training.* Convocation Address at the Bangladesh Open University, Gazipur.

7. Latchem, C. and Henna, D.E. (2002). *Leadership for Open and Learning*. Open Learning. 17 (3). 213 – 215.
8. Pringle, I. and S. Subramanian (2004). Profiles and Experiences in ICT Innovation for Poverty Reduction. Paris: UNESCO.
9. Slater, D. and J. Tacchi (2004). *Research : ICT Innovations for Poverty Reduction*. Paris : UNESCO.
10. UNDP (1995). *Declaration of the Social Development Summit, Copenhagen*, New York, UN.
11. UNDP (2005). *Human Development Report 2004*, New Delhi, OUP.
12. UNESCO (2005). *Education for All: The Quality Imperative*. EFA Global Monitoring Report. Paris: UNESCO.
13. UNESCO (2005). ICT for Capacity Building. Critical Success Factors. 11-13 May 2005.
14. UNESCO (2005). *World Report: Towards Knowledge Societies*. Paris : UNESCO.
15. United Nations (2005). *World Summit Outcome*. New York: UN.
16. World Bank (2005). *World Development Report 2004*. New Delhi, OUP.

9

Human Rights Education from Theory to Practice

United Nations "Peace-building" operations offer new and promising opportunities to develop and apply a general approach to human rights education. An example of this potential is the education, information, and training programme of the Human Rights Component of the United Nations Transitional Authority in Cambodia (UNTAC), The peace plan, under which the United Nations went to Combodia in 1992-93, provided a broad mandate that called for a concentrated and intense effort to carry out human rights education at all levels and of all types. The experience is instructive not only for other possible peace operations under UN auspices, but also as a test case for conceiving a strategy for human rights education and carrying in out under severe time constraints, It is thus a case of a comprehensive approach toward human rights education in both theory and practice.

A new direction of operational support for human rights education emerged with the Security Council's decisions to implement comprehensive political settlement to regional conflicts and its recognition that human rights could provide the normative framework for institutional modifications and constitutional reform, as well as self-determination through free and fair elections. There are three recent examples where education about human rights was given an explicit place in the mandates of UN operations, namely, those in EI Salvador, Cambodia, and Haiti. This is a new dimension on UN peacekeeping since human rights was absent from peacekeeping as traditionally practiced before the late 1980s. Peacekeeping operations did not include either monitoring human rights or informing populations about these rights. With the end of the cold war and the greatly enhanced expectations placed on the United Nations, unfettered by the veto that had blocked so many possible responses to complex emergencies, the Security Council referred more and more frequently to human rights.

The framework for UN peace operation is set out in An Agenda for peace, produced in response to the historic summit of heads of state and government on January 31, 1992. The report defines and reviews the tree traditional areas of preventive diplomacy. Peacemaking, and peacekeeping, plus a fourth, called "Post-conflict peace-building." Whereas preventive diplomacy seeks to avoid the outbreak of a violent conflict, peace building seeks to prevent its recurrence. Designed for situations like EI Salvadoer and Cambodia, where warring parties agree to end hostilities and work toward reconciliation and rehabilitation, but remain suspicious of each other and politically ambitious, peace building should include, in the words of the secretary general, "disarming the previously warring parties and the restoration of order, the custody and possible destruction of weapons, repatriating refugees, advisory and training support for security personnel, monitoring elections, advancing efforts to protect human rights, reforming or strengthening governmental institution and promoting formal and informal process of political participation"? This function also can entails "Support for the transformation of deficient national structures and capabilities and for the strengthening of new democratic institution," in shout "the construction of new environment", "Human rights education within the framework of peace building has been tested in several major UN operations, especially in UNTAC. This chapter examines the application of peace building through human rights education as practices by the United Nations in Cambodia and suggests some general guidelines for human rights education as part of peace building.

UNTAC was an experiment in implementing a broad mandate to reach all levels of society during a brief period. The official duration of the transitional period was just under two years, but the effective period for implementing this mandate was approximately one year. It was an impossibly short period to transform a society, yet a degree of democratic empowerment of occurred and is continuing to affect the political process in Cambodia. To review this experience, I begin with the mandate, that is, what the parties and the UN Security Council asked UNTAC to do, and then discuss how, on the basis of that mandate, a strategy for a countrywide human rights education programme was implemented. With this mandate and strategy in mind, I make some general observations about the opportunities and obstacles facing internationally managed human rights education through the formal and informal structures.

UNTAC's Human Rights Education Mandate and Strategy

The mandate of UNTAC's human rights education programme is set out in the Paris Peace Agreement of October 1991 and Report of the Secretary General of February 1992. The Secretary General's report to the Security Council on Cambodia says that "The development and dissemination of a human rights education programme is foreseen as the cornerstone of UNTAC's activities in fostering respect for human rights.", This statement is based on UNTAC's responsibility as set out in Article 16 of the Paris Agreement for "fostering an environment in which human rights shall be ensured" and Section E of Annex I, which says that UNTAC shall make provision for "development and implementation of a programme of human rights education to promote respect for and understating of human rights, "The meaning of "education" is broad; it implies "teaching" in formal and informal learning environments, as well as "training" and "information". With respect to formal teaching, the Secretary General's report envisaged "that UNTAC would also work closely with existing educational administrative structures in Cambodia to ensure that human rights education is appropriately included in the curriculum at all levels. Including children, adults and special groups" (para 13) significantly the report states that:

Cambodians must fully understand both the content and the significance of those rights and freedoms in order to be in a position to know when and how to protect them properly. This is especially important in an environment in which the framing of a new Cambodian Constitution containing human rights guarantees will be on the national agenda.... Such a civic education programme would be developed in a manner that is culturally sensitive and generally "accessible" to Cambodians, its dissemination would reply upon all channels of communication available in the country. Included printed materials (words and pictures) cultural events and presentations, radio and television media, videocassette distribution mobile teaching units, etc., (para 12-13).

"Training" is also used in the human rights section of the Secretary-general's report in four places:" Complementary training" to civic education (para.14); "some training" in the application of guidelines and materials targeted to civil servants (para.16); "supplementary training" for law enforcement officials and the judiciary, "especially in the areas of fundamental criminal procedure" (para.17) and "Training" of UNTAC personnel in the area of law enforcement and judicial functions (ibid). The term "training" is intended in these passages in the proper sense of imparting skills necessary for the performance of certain specialized tasks.

Thus while the Secretary General's report does not make the distinction between types and levels of education. It does providing guidance on training and information and target groups for these educational activities. The implementation of these broad guidelines required a more specific strategy and plan of action.

After determining that the mandate included all levels and types of education, the Human Rights Component devised and implemented a six-step strategy. Step one was to identify the target groups to whom educational activities would be directed, on the basis of studies of Cambodian Society made by specialized agencies and programmes (such as United Nations Educational, Scientific and Cultural Organisation (UNESCO], the United Nations Children's Fund [UNICEF], and the United Nations Development Programme [UNDP]), consultations with international NGOs, with experience in Cambodia, and Cambodian staff members and indigenous NGOs. The fifteen groups thus targeted included two from UNTAC (UNTAC Civil Police and electoral staff). Seven from the existing administrative structures (police, teachers, university students, ministerial official, other civil servants, political party representatives, judges and prosecutors); and six from the civil society (defenders, human rights associations, women's associations, journalists, monks, and health professionals).

Notably absent from the target groups within the civil society were trade unions. The reasons were that, as confirmed by consultations with the International Labour organisation and the Asian American Free Labour Association, the labour movement was neither independent nor sufficiently organized to provide a context for learning activities. The military, both UN forces and those of the existing administrative structures, was initially included. The Cambodian troops were to be cantoned in special sites where course would be organized. However, the failure to implement the demobilization and cantonment phase of the peace plan excluded this possibility. Nevertheless, in cooperation with the dissemination unit of the local delegation of the International Committee of the Red Cross, several provincial human rights officers setup ad hoc training for the military.

The second element of this strategic planning was a determined the specific expectations with respect to each group and in light of the Secretary General's report. In most cases, the main goal was a basic understanding of the concepts of human rights, the content of the international standards, their applicability to Cambodia, and their relations to the lives and work of the learners.

The third step was to assemble the necessary human and financial resources beyond the initial staff of four in the Education, Training, and Information Unit in Phnom Penh (a training officer, an information officer, an NGO relations officer, and a unit chief). Eventually the Phnom Penh staff assigned to the Education, Training and information Unit was increased by five (two police trainers, one education, officer in charge of women's projects, a training officer to head the mobile teams, and a senior advisor for media projects). Eventually aided by four training assistance and two UN volunteers. A major staffing addition, not foreseen in the Secretary General's report was the appointment in late 1992 of twenty one provincial human rights officers, whose responsibilities included education, training, and information, and twenty one training assistants Khmer speaking educators, trained by the Component and assigned to each provincial human rights officer, working full time on training at the provincial level. Such staffing is reality small compared with other components of the mission, but is significant compared to what is normally available for human rights education.

To supplement the financial resources UNTAC launched an appeal to governments in October 1992, which resulted in a Trust Fund for a Human rights Education programme in Cambodia, with about $1.8 million eventually expended to contract services among local and international NGOs having specialized staff and experience to target groups that component staff were unable to train directly.

The fourth and fifth steps consisted in setting a timetable for each of the projects and implementing them. There was a sense of urgency to proceed with the implementation because of the extremely short time available to the mission, and the conviction that such resources and political will were not likely to be found again, Moreover, bureaucratic delays to obtain approvals from administrative and financial services in Phnom Penh and New York shortened even more the effective time for project implementation.

The sixth and final step was project evaluation, which varied from one project to the next and often took the minimal form of questionnaires completed by participants or a self-evaluation session. Evaluation was more systematic with the police training, law school, health professionals, teacher training colleges, and women's groups. In general, the degree of assimilation of concepts and skill appears directly proportional to the links established between the content of teaching and the daily lives of the learners. Statistic was maintained of the various training activities, although this should be done more systematically in future operations and outside evaluator should be employed. This six-step strategy was implemented in both formal and informal education.

Formal Education

When UNTAC arrived, education in Cambodia was at a virtual standstill, 75 per cent of the teachers, about 67 per cent of primary and secondary level students, and almost 80 per cent of higher education students having been eliminated or fled the country. Formal education facilities had all been closed down or put to other use. It was in this context that UNTAC sought to develop teaching and training on human rights in the schools and universities. Using a slightly different approach for each.

Even where formal education is grossly deficient, the development of human rights education requires working through existing structures. Thus UNTAC obtained from Ministry of Education a decree making human rights part of the official curriculum of civic education in the primary and lowe secondary schools and instructing the provincial education directors to cooperate with provincial human rights officers in setting up programmes in the schools. UNTAC printed teaching materials, conducted briefings and courses for teachers in the schools and in the teacher training colleges, sent mobile teams to the various provinces to give courses of one to two weeks to various groups, and supported several projects directed at primary and secondary education through the Trust Fund.

The university audience was highly receptive to human rights teaching? UNTAC's human rights education efforts focussed primarily on law and medical students. At the country's only law school. UNTAC prepared and taught a four-hour a week course for a three-month period for some 242 students, culminating in an examination. Student motivation and learning curve were both remarkably high in spite of their low level of preparation. Students were particularly receptive to teaching methods that employed critical thinking (not typical in the university) that they could apply to other subjects in law school, rather than the exegesis of abstract international texts. To succeed this method has to place the academic value of free inquiry ahead of the diplomatic propensity to avoid controversial political issues. Teaching, even through the United Nations has little impact if it is based on cautiously worded official positions.

It requires a willingness to link human rights concepts to real-life situations. By taking on an issue on which passions run high in Cambodia (such as the presence of ethnic Vietnamese), students were trained in a four step mode of analysis: (1) Establish the facts impartially; and thoroughly (2) identify the human rights issues involved;

(3) analyze each human rights issue in light of the fact situation; and (4) make appropriate policy recommendations. The most difficult step was the first, since Cambodian students have very little experience with critically assessing sources of information, in part because impartial and reliable information is scarce and in part because "facts" are often created to fit preconceived conclusions. Dr. Allen Keller and his colleagues had similar experiences as the Medial Faculty and the college of Nursing during the projects described in Chapter 21 of this book.

Informal Education

The strategy for "informal education had to be tailored to meet the need and circumstances of each of the target groups. Part of the training, especially in the first months of mission, was directed at UNTAC itself, through briefings for civil police and district electoral supervisors. However, the component's main human rights education effort was directed towards the Cambodian population. In particular, efforts were made through training to reach the key categories of the emerging civil society and public officials and through the media to reach all segments of the population.

The mandate state that "UNTAC would also work closely with...special groups, [including] those individuals best placed to be further disseminators of information such as teachers and community leaders". This section of the mandate was interpreted to mean that human rights education should be directed toward democratic empowerment of the emerging civil society and public officials. The principal forces of civil society in Cambodia are the Buddhist clergy, the free press, and NGOs, mainly those focussing on human rights, women and development.

The Buddhist clergy constitute a particularly effective vehicle for reaching the public at large, especially in remote areas. Buddhism and the monks were severely victimized during the Khmer Rouge period. According to a leading authority on the period, "Khmer Rouge policy toward Buddhism constituted one of the most brutal and through going attacks on religion in modern history" The population of monks was reduced from about sixty thousand to less than one thousand. The Vietnamese installed government in Phnom Penh tolerated the monks, although the National Front for Construction and Defence, an organ of the party, supervised them closely. After arrival of the United Nations, Buddhism flourished and several monks who returned from exile became leaders in the human rights movement. For example, the venerable Mahan Ghosannda, the Supreme Patriarch and Co-founder of the Inter Religious Mission for peace in Cambodia, is an inspirational figure among NGOs. He and his fellow monks found full compatibility between the teachings of the Buddha and international human rights, the following meditation typifies his view that human rights are universal.

During his lifetime, the Buddha lobbied for peace and human rights. We can learn much from a lobbyist like him. Human rights begin when each man becomes a brother and each woman becomes a sister, when we honestly care for each other. Then Cambodians will help Jews, and Jews will help Africans, and Africans will help others. We will all become servants for each other's rights...Any real peace will not favour East, West North or South. A peaceful Cambodia will be friendly to all. Peace is non-violent, and so we Cambodians will remain non-violent towards all as we rebuild our country. Peace is based on justice and freedom, and so a peaceful Cambodia will be just and free.

Through marches, teaching, lobbying with governmental and parliamentary leaders, and spiritual guidance to the populations, which is 90-95 per cent Buddhist, the clergy has popularized constitutionalism and human rights, even in remote areas. During the first year of UNTAC, the Phnom Penh authorities resisted the Component's attempts to set up systematic training for this category. The active participation of monks in the human rights associations, including regularly providing meeting and office space in the WATS (Pagodas), nonetheless allowed the Component to work with them in human rights education. In early 1993 it became possible to implement a more systematic strategy through a Trust Fund project that trained "master trainers" who in turn prepared hundred of monks to teach human rights to their congregations.

The experience with the monks has implications for human rights education in other peace building contexts. With the exception of societies where organized religion is subservient to repressive government, the main religions provide both a source of understanding of prevailing values and a cultural context which must be integrated into teaching. Religions are thus a vehicle for reaching widely and deeply into society. It is unfortunate that this book does not contain a chapter illustrate its importance. No doubt certain intolerant interpretations of major religions and practices of most religions are problematic for human rights, but there is support for the claim that "Faith in human rights education through religious beliefs enormous.

Journalists were already receiving through a UNESCO programme, funded by the Danish government, as well as though the University of Phnom Penh under an arrangement with the French government. The component integrated human rights teaching significantly into these programmes. The UNESCO programme was primarily aimed at skills development for the journalists from all three factions and representing both prints and broadcast journalism. The most common substantive theme of their sessions was human rights, including issues of freedom of expression and human rights aspects of current events in Cambodia. Freedom of expression was generally respected during the transitional period, and there was hope that it would continue to thrive under the new constitution of September 23, 1993 which guarantees freedom to express opinions and to publish (Article 41), some twenty newspapers are published in Khmer, English, French, and Chinese, Some of which criticize the government and its leader freely. Subsequently developments relating to a new press law, the closing of newspapers, and the murder of a journalist have placed these accomplishments in jeopardy. Nevertheless, the international and domestic preoccupation with such incidents is a sign that serious debate over freedom of the press is taking place.

The Cambodian experience illustrates two dimensions of the relation between human rights education and journalism that are more generally, relevant. First regarding the status and freedoms of journalists, it is essential that human rights education activities that reach journalists, civil servants, the police, politicians and NGOs focus attention of the distinction between protected and prohibited speech, and on the rights and responsibilities of journalists, In this field the accusation of imposing Western values should be a matter of open discussion rather than an inhibiting factor. Examples abound to illustrate how in non-western societies, a free press can be the rampart of the civil society against authoritarian rule and a critical element of democratic empowerment.

The second dimension of the relations between human rights education and journalism is that journalists themselves have much to learn about how to report a human rights story. UNESCO had it right in Cambodia by brining human rights concepts into skills training. The persistent lack of professional ethics and skills among Cambodia journalists demonstrates the need to sustain this effort well beyond the short duration of the peace mission. A comprehensive human rights education programme should not tell journalists to preach human rights but rather equip them to identify the rights and remedies relevant to a story. It should always be remembered that these issues are literally matters of life and death in most countries where peace building takes place.

According to the Secretary General's report, "UNTAC would also expect to collaborate with non-governmental organisation (NGOs) operating in Cambodia for this purpose as well as to encourage the establishment of indigenous human rights associations". The proliferation of NGOs independent of the state and party structures, was described by the special representative of the secretary general on human rights in Cambodia as the "first step towards a civil society in Cambodia after its destruction between 1975 and 1975" During the transitional period, UNTAC handled the registration of associations and was quite liberal in accepting applications. Indigenous human rights association and women's organisation were both partners and learners in the component's human rights education effort.

Five human rights groups were functioning in Cambodia during the transitional period, with combined membership claimed to be in the hundreds of thousands. The component focussed its efforts on capacity building so that these groups could become effective advocates and defendants of human rights. Members of these associations were trained as human rights educators, defenders, and monitors. They were provided with materials to conduct their own educational work and participated in component sponsored conferences. Seminars and discussion groups where they could refine their policies and strategies. The key organisation were allotted substantial grants from the UN Trust Fund to organise their own education and training programme and to send delegation to the UN Commission on Human Rights and the Bangkok Preparatory Conference for the World Conference on Human Rights.

A major objective of this support was to mobilize international and regional NGOs to work with their Cambodian counterparts. One of the trust fund projects, the Human Rights task force for the Cambodian elections, was under the responsibility of one U.S., based and six Asian based human rights groups. The task force prepared human rights activists from each of the main indigenous human rights associations to monitor human rights during the election. As a result these associations provided by far the largest numbers of elation observers registered by the Electoral Component. The task force facilitated planning and coordination of activities of these groups and was so successful at this effort that it was continued after the elections as the Cambodian Human Rights Task Force with additional funding from the Trust Fund.

Women's NGOs were also active partners in human rights education. Women constitute more than 60 per cent of the Cambodian population as a result of mass murder and civil war. The lack of equal educational and employment opportunities had deep cultural roots, which required special efforts in human rights education. Courses were run by the component in Phnom Penh and in the provinces, providing both basic educations (introduction to concepts) are in depth "training of trainers" for these associations. They were also provided with trust fund grants to conduct their own human rights education activates or to work with international NGOs. For example an innovative project was conducted with support from the Trust Fund by the Decade of Human Rights Education. (This programme is described in the Chapter by Donna Hicks in this Book.)

After UNTAC's departure, human rights associates continued to be a vital part of Cambodian social and political life. Seven more human rights NGOs have emerged. UNTAC had supported the creation of a coalition of fourteen human rights, women's, and development NGOs, called Ponleu Khmer, which was particularly active during the drafting of the constitution. Ponleu Khmer continued after the proclamation of the constitution and the departure of UNTAC to educate the population about participatory democracy and to push for a sense of accountability on the part of elected officials and civil servants. In June 1994, nine human rights NGOs founded the Cambodian Human Rights Coordination

Committee in order to strengthen links and improve exchanges of information. In 1994 the Cambodian Institute of Human Rights Finalised and obtained official approval of the new human rights curriculum for grades 1 to 11 and organised four-month long constitutional workshops for professors at the law school, government leaders, members of the Assembly, persons trained in law and judges, in an effort to help them better understand the constitution and take it more seriously.

Specific references was also made in the Secretary General's report to officials of existing administrative structures, and in particular police, judges, prosecutors, and civil servants. The Component's strategy was to make officials aware of the obligations the parties had accepted in the peace process and their specific responsibilities as public servants. The second objective was to prepare them for a more responsible and accountable public service under the government to be created following the adoption of the constitution. The strategy was implemented by provincial and Phnom Penh staff of the Component rather than through the Trust Fund. Two police trainers were added to the staff, as was one person experienced in working with civil servants.

With respect to judges and prosecutors, the Component worked with UNTAC's Civil Administration Component on joint training activities following the adoption, in September 1992, of the Provisions Relating to the Judiciary and Criminal Law and procedure Applicable in Cambodia during the Transitional Period (Transitional Provisions). Component staff took part as instructors in courses held for the judges and prosecutors and developed a special series of judicial training activities. In July 1993 a three-week, all-day programme on the judicial functions and independence of the judiciary was organised by the Centre for the independence of judges who had been or were likely to be appointed to the Court of Appeals and the Supreme Court.

Complementing the training of judges was the preparation of persons to represent the accused in court. The near total elimination of all lawyers during the 1975-78 period and thirteen years of one-party rule from 1979-1992 left Cambodia without anything resembling a bar association. No private attorneys or public defenders and practiced in the country in any capacity since 1975. The transitional Provisions guaranteed the right to legal assistance for any persons accused of a crime or a misdemeanour. Because of the dearth of attorneys, the Traditional Provisions stipulated that anyone with a secondary school diploma, or a family member of the accused, regardless of level of education, may represent the accused in court. In order to provide a minimal level or competency for these potential "defenders", the Defenders Training Programme was created, which has continued as a project of the International Human Rights Law Group.

Civil Servants participated in the two-week, courses run by the mobile teams. Many were employed by the local administration without being party members and, in fact, were sympathetic to indigenous human rights NGOs, although they did not reveal this fact to their employers. Separate and specialized course were developed for the Police, who were surprisingly receptive to the training, Interactive and student cantered teaching methods worked well with his group. Of course police training can only have an impact when conducted over the long-term where there is the political will and the institution infrastructure to sustain a professional police accountable to elected representatives.

The experience of human rights education for public officials in Cambodia suggests three considerations of more general relevance. The first is that local authorities are likely to accept training of their officials only if it is handled by international officials. Trainers should be UN staff, even if on temporary status. Second, civil servants relate human rights to their professional work when there is an official code of professional conduct. Of course, the UN Code of Conduct for law Enforcement Officials is the appropriate reference for police training. Other codes should be used for other categories of public officials, such as the basic principles on the Independence of the judiciary and similar texts for prosecutors and the legal profession. Their especially in societies that have undergone years of civil war and political repression, human rights education during the presence of a UN mission can only be the first step in a much longer process of systematic training. Therefore, human rights education should seek, during the mission, support for the planning and financing of training institutes in particular a judicial training institute and a civilian police academy.

A common feature of human rights training in both the civil society and among public officials was a hunger for knowledge about human rights. Past experience with violent conflict and a genuine conviction that the peace building will bring about a more just society undoubtedly contributed to the ready acceptance of major human rights education initiatives by local officials. These conditions, which are likely to exist in other peace-building operations, suggest that those in charge of implementing human rights education should act rapidly and develop ambitious projects that take full advantage of the opening provided by the existing administrative structures.

In developing a strategy for human rights information, the component's task was to develop a culturally relevant human rights information, the Component's task was media. Cultural relevance meant that the message to be disseminated would be consonant with concepts and principles of Cambodian society today. These concepts and principles were found in the Buddhist religion, which provides a spiritual basis for human rights action. The component, in close Collaboration with the TV and Graphic Design units of UNTAC's Information and Education Divisions, developed a human rights information campaign on two pillars, printed materials and audio-visual media.

As regards print media, Khmer artists were used to develop a logo representing a Cambodian landscape with the sunlight of human rights illuminating all aspects of Cambodian life in peace. It was used on T-shirts, Posters, and book covers, such as the cover of a special Khmer edition of the Universal Declaration of Human Rights.

The production and distribution of printed materials served there purposes. Several items were used for teaching, such as the four hundred thousand training leaflets. The compilation of Khmer translations of official UN texts, a found hundred-page book of which 100,000 copies were distributed, served as legal reference for NGOs, defenders, and public officials. Most of the material were aimed at creating a positive including 500,000 basic leaflets 200,000 stickers, 100,000 copies of the Universal Declaration 100,000 balloons and 82,000 posters, specifically the message of these materials was that peace in Cambodia must be built on respect for human rights.

The strategy for broadcast media coved both television and radio, which are particularly important in High of the low level of education and literacy in Cambodia. The human rights "message" was simplified as such as possible and made attractive by using symbols, stories and popular actors. The dissemination of audio-visual materials was done through all existing channels. Video and audio-cassettes were offered to all Cambodian broadcast authorities as well as those outside Cambodia with Khmer programmes directed at Cambodia. In addition, five hundred cassettes with a human rights video were distributed through district electoral supervisors, provincial human rights officers, and indigenous human rights groups, feedback from these circles in dictates that frequent showings were organized even in the remotest areas. UNTAC's ratio and television production units ran into numerous delays but eventually had considerable reach. Radio UNTAC, for example, began in October 1992, producing only one thirty minute programme of "news" (i.e.

excerpts from the UN spokesman's daily briefing), but by election time in May 1993 managed to broadcast fifteen hours a day for seven days a week". Remote areas were reached by twice-daily transmission from voice of America from Bangkok and by distribution by the electoral component in the provinces of a hundred copies of each Ratio UNTAC Programme.

The presence of a peace-building mission generates high expectations among the general population, virtually guaranteeing enthusiastic participation in special events organized them. International Human rights Day offers an ideal opportunity for massive public participations, as was the case on December 10,1992 when the Component, organized celebration throughout Cambodia, with songs, drama productions, speeches by human rights organizations, and distribution of Khmer-language banners, stickers, posters, leaflets, and the brochure containing the Universal Declaration. A poster contest was organized for children under fifteen on "what human rights means to me "resulting in ten thousand posters, the best of which were published, along with selected texts in English and Khmer on Children's rights, in a book called A Dream of Peace. The role of culture is essential to transmission of knowledge and understanding, and traditional means of cultural expression should be a part of a human rights education strategy. UNTAC, with UNESO, produced a series of traditional musical performances, comic books, and series of posters.

The impact of informal training activities and of the mass distribution of printed materials and of television, video, and radio productions has not been tested scientifically. UNTAC estimated that approximately 120,000 people directly benefited from education and training and that the figure for mass communication, considering the population of more than 9 million, the wide availability of radios, the area covered by transmission, and the dissemination of cassettes of the programmes, is probably several million. There are many signs that the basic message that people in Cambodia have certain rights that must be respected by all has penetrated. One year after UNTAC's departure, observes in Cambodia note that the concept and the primacy of human rights have become part of the public discourse in Cambodia to a degree previously unknown.

Conclusions—lessons Learned

The lessons of approximately one year of implementing a programme of human rights education, training, and information in Cambodia are relevant more generally to human rights education as a component of peace building. These lessons concern primarily: (*a*) the definition of target groups; (*b*) the relationship between human rights as taught and practical realities of daily life; (*c*) relations with the exiting administrative structures; (*d*) methods of teaching (*e*) administration of extra budgetary funds for educational projects; and (*f*) long-term impact of education and training.

The strategy described above proved to be successful insofar as the principal elements of Cambodian society were identified and constituted the major transmitters of knowledge and understanding. What is important to consider in developing strategies for other contexts is to persevere whenever to key target groups has been identified but programme actions have been difficult to implement. For example, it was not until fairly late in the mandate of UNTAC that the Component found appropriate implementing agencies to bring human rights education to health professionals and the Buddhist clergy on a significant scale. Had this not been done, there would have been major gaps in the programme.

Teaching, especially at the beginning of UNTAC's human rights programme, tended to describe the relevance of Buddhist principles and then explain the content of the Universal Declaration and the International Covenants. Student's questions led the instructors to realise that effective education must be linked to the lives of the learners.

Moreover, the brevity of the courses meant that this newly acquired knowledge had title chance of being consolidated and transformed into appropriate actions to protect and exercise those rights. Real case studies of violations, for example, have a greater impact than abstract examples. The Women's training Project, in which training was based on Women using drawings and drama to bring out aspects of their daily lives, was the prototype of this approach. The defender's course is another example of an educational activity that is effective when the students are exposed to real courtroom situations.

The local authorities manifested a general willingness not to interfere with practically prepared for such openness, and similar operations should be prepared to move massively into intensive, educational activity. In practice, the opportunities were limited by the availability of staff and funds. Had these two matters been resolved earlier, greater advantage could have been taken of this openness?

There is no doubt that this components programme and other similar ones conducted by the Cambodian human rights associations were successful in that they introduced large number of people for the first time to basic human rights concepts. Support for these groups and retraining of their trainers are essential to the long-term effectiveness of their efforts. The use of mobile teams is an effective mechanism for mass education at a basic level, but they did not have a systematic inbuilt mechanism for ensuring that the critical follow-up work with course participants would be carried on. Video should be used more frequently, especially in villages, where literacy is low. The most important lesson regarding teaching, methods is that, even in a society like Cambodia where people, especially women, are not generally demonstrative, interactive methods work best. This requires more preparation by the teachers but the results are worth it.

The availability of resources through the Trust fund was a vital element in the effectiveness of the programme. It would have been considerably more effective if funds had been available sooner and if the administrative procedure were not as heavy as they were. The availability of such a fund at the beginning would have made a considerable difference.

Finally human rights education, like all other aspects of peace building, is primarily a means of laying long-term foundations for humane governance. The concept of democratic empowerment is helpful as a criterion for conceiving and implementing human rights education projects. This concept is based on a concern for the degree to which the beneficiaries of the project acquire knowledge and skills they can use to participate effectively in decisions affecting their lives. Democratic empowerment of the new government requires assistance in the preparation of key legislation and development and strengthening of national institution. This has been the direction of the successors to the Component, the Phnom Penh office of the UN Centre of Human Rights. In sum, human rights education was tested as part of United Nations pears building in Cambodia on a scale that was unprecedented. Many of the lessons of that experience can be applied elsewhere, if the political will exists to make use of the methods developed by UNTAC in Cambodia and to adapt approaches identified elsewhere in this book to the harsh realities of societies in transition from civil war and political repression to democracy and the rule of law.

REFERENCES

1. See Philip Alston "The Security Council and Human Rights; Lessons to be learned from the Iraq-Kuwait Crisis and Its Aftermath," *Australian Year Book of International law* 13(1992); 107-76.
2. UN General Assembly, Report of the Secretary General on the work of the Organization, An Agenda for Peace; Preventive Diplomacy, Peacemaking and Peacekeeping. *UNDoc A /47/277/* S/24111 (June 17, 1992).32.

3. *Ibid.,* 33-34.
4. According to the Paris Agreement on a Comprehensive Political Settlement of the Cambodia Conflict, the Transitional Period extended from the signing of the agreement (October 23, 1991) to the transfer of authority from the Constituent Assembly to the New Government (September 24, 1993).
5. Report of the Secretary General on Cambodia, *UN Doc.* S/23613 Para 12m this document is the principal source, after the text of the Paris Agreements, of UNTAC's mandate.
6. UNESCO, Inter-sectoral Basic Needs Assessment Mission to Cambodia 15 January-8, February 1991, Report, Bangkok (February 1991) 10.
7. Part of the explanation for the intense interest of university students in human rights is the brutal repression of student demonstrations in 1991, shortly before the arrival of UNTAC.
8. Sometimes, a distinction is made between "informal" and "non-ormula" education. For simplicity, I use "informal" for all types of learning that takes place outside the official schools and universities.
9. Report of the Secretary General, S/23613, Para 13.
10. David Hawk, "The Photographic Record", in Cambodia 1975-1978. Rendervous with Death, ed.Karl D. Jackson (Princeton: Princeton University Press, 1989), 212.
11. *Ibid.*
12. Eva Mysliwiec, Punishing the poor, the International Isolation of Kampuchea (Oxford: Oxfam, 1988). 47.
13. Maha Ghosananda, Step by Step (Berkeley, Calif.: Parallax Press.1992), 70-71.
14. Robert Traer, Faith in Human Rights; Support in Religious Traditions for a Global Struggle (Washington, D.C., Georgetown University, Press, 1991), 219.
15. Report of the Special Representative of the Secretary General, Mr. Michael Kirby (Australia), on the Situation of Human Rights in Cambodia, submitted in Accordance with Commission Resolution 1999-96, *UN Doc. E*/CN.4 / 1994/73 (February 24,1994) para 159 p.41.
16. See Bala Chandran, "Cambodia–Media: Free Press Blurs as Editor Goes to Jail", Inter Press Service, July 27, 1994, p. 15.

17. Report of the Secretary General S/23613 para 13.
18. Report of the Social Representative para 165 p. 42.
19. Report of the Secretary General para.6
20. Zhou mei, Radio UNTAC of Cambodia, Winning Ears, Hearts and Minds (Bangkok, white lots, 1994) 28.
21. Report of the Secretary General, Situation of Human Rights in Cambodia, *UN Doc.* A/49/635 / Add.1 (November 3, 1994), Paras 10-33, pp. 4-10.

10

Determining the Human Excellence

Indian schools and teachers should come out from their tunnel vision of conventional; teaching, Indian organizations have already started adopting many manufacturing and technological inputs from abroad. To match these things, Indian schools and college should also concentrate on such ideas as multiple intelligence and Neuron linguistic Programming at the school level.

We are at the end of this millennium looking forward to the expectation and excitement the nest millennium is going to offer. Lot of changes has taken place leading one to guess the type of changes that are going to take place in the next century. The world has become very competitive. The competition has also ushered in huge opportunities for any one who is willing to prepare oneself to exploit the same. In this context, the issue of preparing our students to meet the challenges of the nest millennium be comes very critical.

The approach to education and personality development has taken a very different dimension during this century. Parents dimension during this century. Parents are very keen to make their children assume grater responsibilities in their lives. Great emphasis is given for imparting quality education for their wards. The single purpose of education and curriculum development can only be towards preparing the student to partake in the excitement of the next century.

World over, the emphasis on education has been shifting from not only academic excellence but also to overall excellence. In this context, the concept of Multiple Intelligence is very crucial, to meet the challenges of change, children should be developed in various parameters. Lot of research has taken place in understanding the human excellence. The Brain which is come the center of command for the human system has been studied from various perspectives. One of the researchers is Dr. Howard Gardener, who has done extensive research on human excellence. He defines intelligence as "the ability to solve problem that counters in real life and the ability to generate new problem to solve". He says the human mind should also have the ability to make something or offer a service that is valued within one's culture. He focuses of eight types of intelligences;

(*i*) Linguistic Intelligence

It is the ability of a student to express ideas and concept in words. Communication is going to play a very vital role in the years to come and students should be in a position to express them clearly and succinctly so that they are able to convert their knowledge into usable products. Students who have high level of linguistic intelligence perform very well as writer, speakers and journalists.

(*ii*) Logical Mathematical Intelligence

It is the ability to concentrate on mathematical problems, hypotheses and to think logically. Scientists, accountants, engineers, computer programmers, researchers all have a high level of this intelligence.

(*iii*) Spatial Intelligence

This is a very important skill which will enable a person to think in a three dimensional perspective. It calls for a high level of visual constructed images and creativity in one self.

Student with spatial intelligence have the capacity to become architects, painters or pilots, which call for this skill in the day-to-day application of their work.

(*iv*) Bodily-kinaesthetic Intelligence

This intelligence is the ability to manipulate various things and objects. It also calls for fine tuning physical skills; one would appreciate the extent to which athletes and sportspersons dancers or surgeons.

(*v*) Musical Intelligence

The brain has two halves viz., the left hemisphere and right hemisphere. The left hemisphere is logical, mathematical and linguistic. On the other hand, the right hemisphere is the hemisphere where the music and creativity talents are developed. Students who have a high degree of musical intelligence are high brain driven. These students demonstrate their ability to understand and contribute to music. They can appreciate the parameters such as pitch, melody rhythm or tone. The students who excel in this become leading composer's music directors, music critics or instrument makers. If this intelligence is developed among students, their right brain is activated and they start thinking creatively.

(*vi*) Inter-personal Intelligence

This is the capacity to improve the rapport and people manage skills. In the life of anybody, whatever may be the intelligence and knowledge; if one cannot connect with others they will not be very effective. In this context, inter-personal intelligence becomes very important students who excel in inter-personal intelligence to go as teachers, social workers, politicians or nay one who has to interact with public at large.

(*vii*) Intra-personal Intelligence

It is the ability to introspect and understand oneself in newer dimensions. It also includes the ability to plan ahead and direct one's life students with a very high of intra-personal intelligence are bale to understand their strengths and weaknesses. Student who have this ability become theologians, psychologists, philosophers or original thinkers.

(*viii*) Naturalist Intelligence

It is the ability to understand nature and use the gifts of nature for one's own development. Students with high level of naturalist intelligence of well as agriculturists, farmers, landscapers, etc., It is possible in an educational institution to develop the above eight types of intelligences. With the unfolding of the next century, the opportunities are going to be very wide. In our country, we have been seeing excessive importance in certain disciplines such as engineering, medicine and computer programming.

The world offers equal scope and opportunities in other fields also. For example, there are not many writers, architects, original thinkers or scientists. With the economic reforms and liberalization of the Indian economy, the migration of students to various parts of the world has becomes very common. This means that the students have to be prepared not only for the Indian requirements but also to the world requirements.

India is witnessing the entry of multinational organizations. To succeed in the future business environment is going to be a difficult ball game. If the students are not developed properly to meet the challenges of change, it is going to be very difficult for them to compete in the newly changes order. Many research and application based books are available to develop Multiple Intelligence in a classroom situation. Applying Multiple Intelligence and Neuron Linguistic programming skills in a classroom makes a lot of difference in the quality of life and capabilities of the students. Indian school and teachers should be able to come out from their tunnel vision of conventional teaching> Indian organizations have already started adopting many of the manufacturing and technological inputs from abroad.

To match these things, Indian schools and colleges should also concentrate on such ideas as Multiple Intelligence and Neuron Linguistic programming at the school level. If this is not donning, Indian students will be left behind in the march towards the next millennium in which all other countries are going to participate.

11

Cultural Relativism and Universal Human Rights

Cultural Relativity

Cultural relativity is an undeniable fact, moral rules and social intuitions evidence an astonishing cultural and historical variability. The doctrine of cultural relativism holds that at least some such variations cannot be legitimately criticized by outsiders. But if human rights are literally the rights everyone has simply as a human being, they would seem to be universal by definition. How should the competing claims of cultural relativism and universal human rights be reconciled? I defined an approach that maintains the fundamental universality of human rights while accommodating the historical and cultural particularity of human rights discussed above.

Defining "Cultural Relativism"

What we can call radial cultural relativism would hold that culture is the sole source of the validity of a moral right or rule. Radical universalism would hold that culture is irrelevant to the validity of moral rights and rules. Which are universally valid? The body of the continuum defined by these ideal typical end-points—that is, those positions involving varying mixes of relativism and universalism—can be roughly divided into what we can call strong cultural realism and weak cultural relativism.

Strong cultural relativism holds that culture is the principal source of the validity of a moral right or rule. Universal human rights stand, however, serves as a check of potential excess of relativism at its furthest world extremes, just short of radical relativism, strong cultural relativism would accept a few basic rights with virtually universal application, but allow such a wide range of variation for most rights. Those two entirely justifiable wets might overlap only slightly. Weak cultural relativism holds that culture may be an important source of the validity of a moral right or rule. Universality is initially presumed, but the validity of human nature, communities, and rights serve as a check on potential excess of universalism. At its furthest extreme, just short of radical universalism, weak cultural relativism would recognize a comprehensive set of prima facie universal human rights, but allow occasional and strictly limited local variations and exceptions.

We must be careful not to use merely quantitative measures of relativism; qualitative judgements of the significance of different cultural variations must also be incorporated. In a rough way, three-hierarchical levels of variation can be distinguished, involving cultural relativity in the substance of lists of human rights, in the interpretation of individual rights, and in the form in which particular rights are implemented. As we move "down" the hierarchy, we are in effect further specifying and interpreting (in the ordinary sense of that term) the higher level, and the range of permissible variation at a given level is set by the next higher level. For example: "Interpretations" of a right are logically limited by the substance of a right; even the range of variation in substance is set by the notions of human nature and dignity from which the list of rights derives. I shall ultimately define a weak cultural relativist position that permits deviation from universal human rights standards primarily at the level of form.

Relativity and Universality: A Necessary Tension

The dangers of the moral imperialism implied by radical universalism hardly need be emphasized. Radical universalism is subject to other moral objections as well. Moral rules, including human rights, function within a moral community. Radical universalism requires a rigid hierarchical ordering of the multiple moral communities to which individuals and groups belong. In order to preserve complete universality for human rights, the radical universalism must give absolute priority to the demands of the cosmopolitan moral community over all other ("lower") moral communities.

This complete denial of national and sub national ethical autonomy and self-determination is not acceptable. Even if the nation should prove to be a doomed, transitory stage in the development of human moral community, there is no inescapable logical or moral reason why people cannot accept or choose it as their principal from of social organization and the locus of important extra familial, moral and political commitments. Similar arguments might be made for other communities that do not encompass the entire human race. Once we allow the moral validity of such commitments, we are bound to accept at least certain types of substantive moral variability, including variability in human rights practices. Such moral "nationalism" may be based on political reasons, such as an inability to agree on the structure of a supranational organization, or a fear of creating an instrument of universal tyranny. More directly moral reasons might also be advanced—for example, the advantages of international diversity provided by a strong commitment to national or local customs. Most important, it resets on the notion of self-determination. However it is justified, as at least certain choices of such moral communities demand respect from outsiders—not necessarily uncritical acceptance, let alone emulation, but in some at least, tolerance.

If radical universalism cannot be justifiably maintained—at least with respect to any robust substantive list of human rights, such as the provided in the at Universal Declaration and covenants—even a weak cultural relativist account of human rights seems on its face guilty of logical contradiction. If human rights are based in human nature, on the simple fact that one is a human being, than how can human rights be relative in any fundamental way?

Human Mechanism

The simple answer is that human nature is itself in some measure culturally relative. There is a sense in which this is true even biologically—for example, if marriage partners are chosen of the basis of cultural preference concerning height, weight, hair colour, skin tone, or other physical attributes, the gene pool in a community may be altered in ways that are equivalent to "natural" mechanisms of selection. More important, culture can significantly influence the presence and expression of many less easily quantified aspects of human nature—for example, by encouraging or discouraging the development or perpetuation of certain personality traits and types.

Cultural Variation

Whether we conceive of this process as involving cultural variation around an unalterable core or as cultural variations largely within a physiologically fixed range, there is a social side to human nature that cannot be defined, at least insofar as that nature is expressed. "Human nature" is a range of possibilities varying, in part in response to culture, within certain psycho-biological limits; it is as such a project and an individual and social discovery as it is a given fact. Even if all behaviour should prove to be ultimately genetic, the expression of that genetic endowment in human behaviour—which also merits being called "human nature"—is in considerable measure culturally determined.

Categorical Cultural

The strongest form of radical cultural relativism would hold that the concept "human being" is of no moral significance, that the mere fact that one is a human being" is irrelevant to one's moral status. Many premodern societies have not even recognized "human being" as a descriptive category, but instead defined persons by social status or by group membership. For example, the very names of many cultures mean simply "the people" and their origin myths may define them as separate from outsiders, who are somehow "not-human." Similarly, the ancient Greeks divided the world into Hellenes and barbarians.

Significance of Cultural Values

Even more striking is the apparent cross-cultural consensus dense on a few practices that cannot be justified by even the hoariest of traditions, and certainly not by any few customs. For example, the prohibiting of torture and the requirement of procedural due process in imposing and executing legal punishment seem to be accepted as binding by virtually all cultures, despite profound differences in specifying the practical and substantive meanings of these notions. There is also a striking cross-cultural consensus on many of the values that today we seek to protect through human rights. Especially when those values are expressed in relatively general terms as life, social order, family, and protection from arbitrary rule, and prohibition of inhuman and degrading treatment, the guarantee of a place in the life of the community, and access to an equitable share of the means of subsistence are central moral aspirations in nearly all cultures.

Importance of Relatives

The radical relativist might respond that such consensus is irrelevant. Logically, this is correct; cross-cultural consensus does not necessarily entail any additional force for a moral rule. But most people do believe that such consensus adds force to the rule. So this kind of radical relativism, although logically impeccable, is in an important sense morally defective. In effect, a moral analogue to customary international law seems to operate. If a practice is nearly universal and generally perceived as obligatory, that practice is required of all members of the community, it would impose certain substantive limitations on the range of permissible cultural moral variation.

Rhetorical Devices

Plausible arguments can be advanced to justify alternative mechanisms to guarantee human dignity—for example, nature law, which imposes Tran cultural moral obligations that are not correlative to right. Few in any state, however, actually advance such arguments. In the first, second, and third worlds alike, a strong commitment to human rights is almost universally proclaimed, even where practice throws that commitment into question. And even if such proclamations are mere rhetorical fashion. Such a widespread international moral" fashion" must have some substantive basis.

Moral Values of Human Rights

That basis is the moral hazard presented by the modern state. Traditional rules usually faced substantial moral limits on their political power, customary limits that were entirely independent of human rights and the relative technology and administrative weakness of traditional states and non-state political institutions further restrained arbitrary abuses of power. In such a world, inalienable entitlements of individuals held against state and society might plausibly be held to be superfluous, if not positively dangerous to well-established practices that realised a cultural conception of human dignity.

Such a world exists today only in a relatively small number of isolated areas. And the modern state, particularly in the Third would, not only operates relatively free of the moral constraints of custom but also has far greater administrative and technological reach. It thus represents a serious threat to basic human rights seem necessary rather than optional. In contemporary circumstances, then, radical or universe rifted relativism, is as inappropriate as unrestricted universalism. Some kind of intermediate position is required.

VARIETIES OF CULTURAL RELATIVISM

Internal *Vs.* External Judgements

This distinction between internal and external evaluations roughly corresponds to, and further elaborates, the distinction between strong and weak cultural relativism; the stronger one's relativism, the greater one's reliance on internal evaluations. It also helps to elucidate the dilemma we face in judging culturally specific practices, torn between the demands of relativism and universalism.

Respect for autonomous moral communities would seem to demand internal evaluations, but to rely on internal judgment alone abrogates one's moral responsibilities as a member of the cosmopolitan moral community. Membership in one's own national or local moral community might also demand judgment. Further more, moral judgements are by their nature universal, or at least universalisable, even we know that moral values and particular judgment are at least in part historically specific and contingent.

Evaluation of Cultural

The choice between internal and external evaluations thus is itself a moral choice. Should we abandon an external judgment because a practice has a long and well-established place within another cultural tradition? Our answer to that question should depend in large measure on the moral importance of the practice, from both the external and the internal perspectives, and on the nature of the internal judgment.

We can identify the force underlying such judgment is the inherent universality of basic moral precepts, at least as we understand mortality in the west. We simply do not believe that our moral precepts are for us and us alone. This is most evident in Kantian and other deontological moral theories, but it is no less true of utilitarianism; the principle of utility is explicitly advanced by Bentham and Mill as a universal moral principle. And, of course, nature of human rights theories is also inherently universal. For most of us, morality is inherently universalitistic and egalitarian.

Futhermore, our moral precepts are our moral precepts. As such, they demand obedience of us. To refuse to act on our own precepts simply because others reject them is to fail to give proper weight to our own moral beliefs, at least in the case of central moral precepts, such as the equality of all human beings and the protection of innocents. And no matter how firmly someone else, or even a whole culture, believes differently, at some point we simply must say that those contrary beliefs are wrong. Negative external judgement may be problematic, but in some cases at least they seem not only permissible also demanded.

Relativism in Implementing Human Rights

The distinction between variations in form and in interpretation may be difficult to draw with precision, but it is fairly clean and important. Consider a particular right, such as the right to political participation. In further specifying the right to political participation, we can begin by distinguishing electoral from no electoral, from non-electoral forms of participation. Within the realm of electoral participation, we can distinguish elections based on universal adult suffrage from those based on a suffrage limited by sex, income, or some other such criterion; elections where voting is a right from those where it is a privilege or even a duty; elections intended to determine the will of the people from elections that serve principally to mobilize popular support for government policy, and so forth. These variations in ‘ inter-predation” clearly are qualitatively different from questions of “form” such as how often elections, town meetings, plebiscites, or gatherings of village elders will be held they shall be called.

Conception of Human Rights

Particular human rights are likely “essentially contested concepts” in which there is a substantial but rather general consensus of meaning coupled with a no less important and apparently unresolvable conflict of interpretation. In such circumstances, culture provides one plausible and defensible mechanism for selecting interpretations. Nonetheless, there are strong limits on the acceptable range of variation. Not all “interpretations” however, are equally plausible or defensible. They are interpretations, not free associations or arbitrary stipulations. The meaning of—the right to political participation,” for example, is controversial, but the range of controversy is limited by the substance of the concept: an election in which a people were allowed to choose an absolute dictator for life is simply an indefensible interpretation. Furthermore, even logically valid interpretations are more subject to external criticism than variations in form.

When such priorities are set, an especially extreme emphasis or de-emphasis of a right brings us to the edge of the third type of relativity—namely, variations in substance. Such substantive differences in lists of human rights should rarely be accepted. Rights that vary in form and interpretation still may be “universal” in an important sense if the substantive list of rights can be said to have considerable international normative universality. There may also be a weaker universality even in the midst of considerable substantive diversity—for example, if there is a large common core with relatively few differences “around the edges.” Or if there are strong statistical regularities and the outliers are few, and are clearly overshadowed by the central tendency.

I am what some uncomfortable with the degree of relativity implied by even such an extended notion of "universality" but some such variations are perhaps defensible.

Universal Rights

Another important consideration is the extent to which the listed rights are aggregated. At the level of such broad categories as civil, political, economic, and social rights, there is widespread agreement that "universality" is required; any defensible list must include rights from all these categories. As we disaggregate. However, the permissible range of relativity expands, in part because desegregation is largely a process of interpretation, in a broad sense of that term.

Thus we see once more and in greater detail that we do not face an either—or choice between cultural relativism and universal human rights. Rather, we need to combine the universality of human rights and their particularity, and thus accept a certain limited relativity for even universal human rights.

Culture and Relativism

The cultural basis of cultural relativism must be considered too, especially because numerous contemporary arguments against universal human rights standards strive for the cause of cultural relativism but actually are entirely without culture basis. Standard arguments for cultural relativism rely on such examples as the pre-colonial African village, Native American tribes, and traditional Islamic social systems, but we have seen that human rights are foreign to such communities, which employed other mechanisms to protect and realise human dignity.

Such communities, however, are increasingly the exception rather than the rule. They are not, for example, the communities of the teeming slums that hold an ever-growing proportion of the population of most third world states. Even most rural areas of the Third World have been substantially penetrated, and the local culture 'corrupted,' by foreign practices and institutions, including the modern state, the money economy, and "western" values, products, and practices. In the Third World today we see most often not the persistence of traditional; culture in the face of modern intrusions, or even the development of syncretism cultures and values, but rather a disruptive "westernization" cultural confusion, or the enthusiastic embrace of "modern" practices and values. In other words, the traditional culture advanced to justify cultural relativism far too often no longer exists. But communitarian defence of traditional practices usually cannot be extended to modern nation states and contemporary nationalist regimes.

Therefore, while recognizing the legitimate claims of self-determination and cultural relativism, we must be alert to cynical manipulation of a dying, lost, or even mythical cultural past. We must not be misled by complaints of the inappropriateness of "Western" human rights made by repressive regimes whose practices have at best only the most tenuous connection to the indigenous culture: communitarian rhetoric too often cloaks the depredations of corrupt and often Westernized or deracinated elites.

Argumentative Cultural

Arguments of cultural relativism are far too often made by economic and political elites that have long since left traditional culture behind. While this may represent a fundamentally admirable effort to retain or recapture cherished traditional values, it is at least ironic to see largely Westernized elites warning against the value and practices they have adopted. At their best, such arguments tend to be dangerously paternalistic. For example "villagization," which was supposed to reflect traditional African conceptions, was accomplished in Tanzania only by force, against the vocal and occasionally even violent opposition of much of the population. And even such a troubling sincerity is unfortunately rare.

Arguments of cultural relativism regularly involve urban elites eloquently praising the glories of village life—a life that they or their parents or grandparents struggled hard to escape and to which they have not the slightest intention of returning. Government officials denounce the corrosive individualism of western values—while they line their pockets with the proceeds of massive corruption, drive imported luxury automobiles, and plan European or American vacations. Leaders sing the praise of traditional communities—while they wield arbitrary power antithetical to traditional values. Purse development politicians that systematically undermine traditional communities, and replace traditional leaders with corrupt cronies and party hacks. Such cynical manipulation of tradition occurs everywhere. Let me cite, however, a few examples from Africa, where "some leaders have even resorted to picking out certain elements of traditional African culture to anesthetize the masses. Despite what is said, this frequently has little to do with a return to the positive, authentic dimensions of African tradition"

Other Views

In Malawi, president Hastings Kamuza Banda utilizes "traditional courts' to deal with political opponents outside the regular legal system. For example, Orton and Vera Chirwa, after being kidnapped from Zambia, were brought before a "traditional court" made up of five judges and three tribal chiefs, all appointed directly by Banda. While there was a prosecutor, no defence attorney was allowed, and the only possible appeal was to banda personally. Such procedures have not the slightest connection with authentic traditional practices. In Zaire, President Mobutu has created the authentic traditional basis. In fact, it is essentially a revival of the colonial practice of 'curve labour'. In Niger, Samaries, traditional youth organizations have been "revived," but not so much out of a respect for traditional culture as "to replace party organizations so as channel youthful energies away from polities". And Macias Nguema of Equatorial Guinea, probably the most vicious ruler independent black Africa has seen, called himself "Grand Master of Popular Education, Science, and Traditional Culture," a title that might be comical were the situation not so tragic.

The cynicism of many claims of cultural relativism can also be seen in the fact that far too often they are for foreign consumption only. The same elites that raise culture as a defence against external criticisms based on universal human rights often ruthlessly suppress inconvenient local customs whether of the majority or of a minority. National unification certainly will require substantial sacrifices of local customs, but the lack of local cultural sensitivity shown by many national elites that strongly advocate an international cultural relativism suggests a very high degree of self-interest.

Furthermore, a number of regrettably common practices, such as disappearances, arbitrary arrest and detention, or torture, are entirely without cultural basis. Idi Amin, Pol Pot, and death squads of EI Salvador cannot be attributed to local culture; while these names have become justly synonymous with modern barbarism. Such practices are not an expression of established cultural traditions.

In traditional cultures—at least the kinds of traditional cultures that might justify deviations from international human rights standards—people are not victims of the arbitrary decision of rulers whose principal claim to power is their control of modern instrument of force and administration. In traditional cultures, communal customs and practices usually provide each person with a place in society and a certain amount of dignity and protection. Furthermore, there usually are reciprocal bonds between ruler and ruled and between rich and poor. The human rights violations of most third world regimes are as antithetical to such cultural traditions as they are to

"Western" human rights conceptions. In fact, authentic traditional cultural practices and values can be an important check on abuses of arbitrary power. Traditional African cultures, for example, usually were strongly constitutional, with major customary limits on rules; as a Booth maxim says, "A chief is a chief by the people." Not only are these traditional checks a resource that human rights advocates may be able tap, but it has even been argued that transgressions of traditional limits have figured in the collapse of some recent regimes.

Justification of Cultural

Finally, there are substantive human rights limits on even well-established cultural practices, however difficult it may be to specify and defend particular account of what those practices are. For example, sexual, racial, Ethnic, and religious discriminations have been widely practiced but are indefensible today. Likewise, the depth of the tradition of anti-Semitism in the west is no defence for the maintenance of the practice. This is not to say that certain cultural differences can not justify even fundamental deviations from" universal" human rights standards, but if cultural relativism is to guarantee local self-determination, rather than clock despotism, we must insist on a strong, authentic cultural basis, as well as on the presence of alternative mechanisms to guarantee basic human dignity, before we justify cultural derogations from universal human rights.

Assessing Claims of Cultural Relativism

The internal normative consensus on human rights presents a strong prima facie case for a relatively strong universalism—that is, for weak cultural relativism. Even if this "consensus" is largely the compliment of vice to virtue, it does reveal widely shared notions of "virtue." An underlaying "universal" moral position that compels at least the appearance of assent from even the cynical and corrupt.

Furthermore, as I have argued above, in the conditions of modern society human rights are a particularly appropriate mechanism to protect human dignity. The modern state, the modern economy, and associated "modern" values tend to create communities of relatively autonomous individuals who lack the place and protection provided by traditional society. And regardless of the relative degree of individual autonomy, people today face the particularly threatening modern state and the especially fierce buffeting of the ever-changing modern economy. Rights held equally by all against the state—right, that both limit its legitimate range of action and require positive protection against certain predictable economic, social, and political contingencies—are a seemingly natural and necessary response to typically modern threats to human dignity and basic human values, traditional and modern alike.

Rights are formulate with certain basis violation, or standard threats to human dignity, in mind therefore, the easiest way to overcome the presumption of universality is to demonstrate that the anticipated violation is not standard in that society, that the value is justifiably not considered basis in that society, or that the object of the right is guaranteed by an alternative mechanism. To overcome the presumption of universality, one would have to show that the underlying cultural vision of human nature or society is both morally defensible and incompatible with the implementation of the "universal" human right in question.

Human Rights

Which recognize right to life, liberty, and security of the person; the guarantee of legal personality; and protections against slavery, arbitrary arrest, detention, or exile, and inhuman or degrading treatment. These are so clearly connected to basic cross-cultural requirements of human dignity, and are stated in sufficiently general terms, that any morally defensible contemporary form of social organization must recognize them (although perhaps not necessarily as inalienable rights) I am even tempted to say that conceptions of human nature or society that are incompatible with such rights would be indefensible almost by definition. Such civil rights as freedom of conscience, speech, and association may be a bit more relative. Because they assume the existence and positive evaluation of relatively autonomous individuals, and they may be of questionable applicability in strong, thriving traditional communities.

In such communities, however, they would rarely be at issue. If traditional practices truly are based on and protect culturally accepted conceptions of human dignity, then members of such a community simply will not have the desire or need to claim such civil rights. In the more typical contemporary case, however, in which the relatively autonomous individual faces the modern state, they too would seem to be universally demanded; it is hard for me to imagine a defensible modern conception of human dignity that did not include at least most of these rights. A similar argument can be made for the economic and social rights of the Universal Declaration.

The Declaration does list some rights that are best viewed as "interpretation", subject much grater cultural relativity. For example, the right of free and full consent of intending spouses reflects a specific cultural interpretation of marriage that is of relatively recent origin and by no means universal today, even in the west. Notice, however, that the right is subordinate to the right to marry and to found a family, for which there is a strong cross-cultural consensus.

Finally, we should note that even the strongest cultural relativist faces a particularly serious problem where cultures clash or are undergoing substantial transformation, as is the case in much of the Third world. In evaluating customary practices that involve otherwise justifiable deviations from or interpretations of prima facie universal human rights, we often face the problem of "modern" individuals or groups who reject traditional practices. Should we give priority to the idea of community self-determination and permit the enforcement of customary practices against modern "deviants," even if this violates "universal" human rights? Or should individual self-determination prevail, thus sanctioning claims of universal human rights against traditional society? We return to this issue in chapter 8, but a few brief comments are in order here.

Recent Trends in Women's Rights

In a recent discussion of women's rights in Africa, Rhoda Howard suggests an attractive and widely applicable compromise strategy on a combination of practical and moral grounds. Howard argues against an outright ban on such practices as child betrothal and widow inheritance, but she also argues strongly for national legislation that permits women (and the families of female children) to "opt out" of traditional practices. Where practical, guaranteeing a right to "opt out" of traditional practices in favour of "universal" human rights or alternative human rights interpretations seems ideal, for it permits an individual in effect to choose his or her culture, or the terms on which he or she will participate in the traditional culture.

Conclusion

Conflicting practices, however, may sometimes be irreconcilable for example, a right to private ownership of the means of production is incompatible with the maintenances of a village society in which families hold only right of use to communally owned land; allowing individuals to opt out and fully own their land would destroy the traditional system. Less dramatic, full freedom of religion, including a right to apostasy is incompatible with certain well-established traditional Islamic views. But even such conflict may sometimes be resolved, or at least minimized, by the physical or legal separation of adherents of old and new values. Although separation may be difficult—given the interpenetration of rural and urban sectors, for example—it may be possible, particularly with practices that are not material to the maintenance or essential integrity of either culture.

Nevertheless, a choice must sometimes be made, at least by default, between competing practices or conceptions of human rights. Such cases take us out of the realm in which useful general guidelines are possible. Fortunately though, they are the exception rather than the rule. I believe that we can justifiably insist on some form of weak cultural relativism—that is, a fairly strong universalism. It may be necessary to allow limited cultural variations in the form and interpretation of particular human rights, but we must insist on their fundamental moral universality. Human rights are, to use an appropriately paradoxical phrase, relatively universal.

12

Recognising the Pedagogy of Voice in a Learning Community

Stewart Ranson
School of Education, the University of Birmingham

Introduction

If cities, in the global age, are to address the twin tasks of urban regeneration and social inclusion they will require a renaissance in learning (EC/Fast). This challenge is to develop 'the capabilities' (Sen, 1985; 1990; Nussbaum and Sen, 1994) for citizens to become active participants in remaking the communities in which they live and work. While much public policy focuses upon the skills young people will need to enter and survive in the labour market, less emphasis is accorded to the significance of encouraging them to find the voice and practices of cooperative agency indispensable to flourishing within a democratic civil society.[1]

This paper elaborates an argument being developed in five Education Action Zones (EAZs). The Zones are a policy initiative designed to create the new forms of governance—learning communities of partnership and voluntary

---

[1]The paper builds on Martin 1996, 1999; Ranson, 1992, 1997, 1998; Ranson et al., 1999; Ranson and Stewart, 1994

participation—that can develop the capabilities citizens' need for the task of regenerating civil society.

Social Exclusion as the Denial of Citizenship

Growing concern about increasing unemployment and poverty in Europe from the late 1970s into the 1990s led to the creation of a number of European anti-poverty programmes. Within these programmes a debate began about which vocabulary was appropriate to conceptualize the growing forms of poverty and disadvantage. The discussion tended to reflect different paradigms of analysis. An Anglo-Saxon tradition (Townsend, 1979; Rowntree, 1998) retains the concept of *poverty* as best able to capture the experience of disadvantage: inadequate material resources and income at the disposal of individuals or households and the distributional issues which underlie this lack of resources. The related concept of *deprivation* focuses upon the need to judge poverty in relation to prevailing material standards (of diet, clothing and housing) and services and the need for an adequate minimum standard of living, encompassing income, services and amenities (Oppenheim, 1998).

This discourse has however, been increasingly supplemented by a French and continental discourse of *social exclusion* (Silver, 1994). Here the focus is primarily on relational issues: in other words, inadequate social participation, lack of social integration and lack of power (Room, 1995). For Castells (1990) social exclusion is the process of becoming detached from the moral order of mutual rights and obligations. In an influential report, *Social Exclusion and Human Dignity in Europe,* social exclusion is defined as: 'inability to participate effectively in economic, social, political and cultural life—alienation and distance from the mainstream society' (Duffy, 1995). The emphasis in social exclusion is, therefore, upon *the processes* which lead people to become isolated and marginalized from the mainstream, from what the European Commission has termed the production and distribution of social resources: the labour market, informal networks and the state.

This concept of social exclusion has become increasingly fashionable amongst New Labour think-tanks, attracted by the search for a 'third way' of understanding welfare issues, less in terms of wealth distribution and more in terms of relational processes of human and social capital. A Demos special edition defined social exclusion as 'loss of access to the most important life chances that a modern society offers' through becoming disconnected from jobs, education, homes, leisure, civic organizations and even voting (Perri 6, 1997). In an Institute of Public Policy Research (IPPR) publication, *An Inclusive Society,* Mulgan (1998) recognizes that 'the concept of exclusion is in part about power and agency: people's capacity to control their own lives. It is a dynamic concept about prospects as well as current situations. And, more than concepts of poverty, exclusion is about particular communities and particular societies. It is in this sense historically specific' (p. 260). The solution to these issues lies, he argues, in the reform of governance to promote interdisciplinary and multi-agency working—'joined up', holistic government.

This understanding should, however, lead analysis to consider the structural as well as the processual factors that contribute to social exclusion. Geddes (1997) helpfully illuminates the significance of this distinction: 'the notion of social exclusion (recognizes) that disadvantage is experienced by individuals within local communities, and can be either reinforced by the degeneration of community or moderated by its network of mutual support' (p. 208). This approach has the advantage of achieving a more encompassing defining of exclusion that embraces not only the poor, but all those subject to varying forms of discrimination and segregation (for example, single women, disabled people, minority ethnic groups).

Research thus needs to study the multidimensional aspects of both these relational and distributional characteristics of disadvantage and exclusion (Room, 1995). The processes which exclude communities and individuals are interrelated and a framework of analysis is needed to show their necessary connections. The task, Mingione (1997) proposes, is to integrate the paradigms of poverty and social exclusion by revealing the way they combine to deny the disadvantaged participation in citizenship. This strategy is taken up by some in this country. Poverty undermines citizens self-esteem, expectations, status and power which together erode their sense of well-being and capacity to participate together as members of society (Oppenheim, 1998). Poverty and exclusion are thus best interpreted as twin processes which deny the material, social and political rights of citizenship. Yet to cast the understanding of citizenship in terms of rights alone is now increasingly problematized.

Citizenship: from Rights to Voice

The debate about disadvantage points to the conclusion that to be excluded is to be denied the material and social conditions which allow members of communities to recognize each other as citizens who share a common status and equal rights. Yet, traditional models of 'entitlement citizenship', which emphasize membership of the nation state and formal legal rights (Marshall, 1977; Plant, 1990) have been subjected to critical analysis because they ignore the contemporary condition of plurality (Parekh, 1988) which now gives rise to claims for participation, exercise of agency and deliberation, aspects of citizenship which informed classical traditions but have become neglected (Barber, 1984). The task has been to reconstruct a theory of citizenship which is grounded in the experience of heterogeneity and elaborates the need for different groups to enter a discourse in which they voice claims for their identities and interests to be recognized and accommodated in the public space. Theorists (Young, 1990; Phillips, 1993, 1995; Mouffe, 1992, 1993) point to the mistaken illusion of a unified polity, of homogeneous communities which form a universal citizenry and civic public, which is required to leave behind particularity and difference in the public domain. Traditional models of citizenship imposed a univocal understanding of what should count as 'universal' values that excluded and silenced the voices of 'other' traditions, whether they are gendered, ethnic or class. A conception of citizenship is needed, Yeatman (1994) argues, which acknowledges the contested nature of public purposes and enables the different voices to re-present their cultural traditions and material class interests (Coole, 1996) in the public space in conditions of unconstrained dialogue.

'Voice', typically, expresses the meanings and purposes on actor which is communicated in a variety of written as well as spoken forms. Voice, argues Wertsch (1991), following Bakhtin, 'is concerned with the broader issues of a speaking subject's perspective, conceptual horizon, intention and world view.' Voice in this sense is encapsulated in Habermas' (1984) 'communicative action' or Austin's (1962) 'speech acts': the perspectives expressed in communication are constructed to construct and influence the course of social action (cf. Hirschmann, 1970).

An inclusive citizenship thus requires 'recognition' of different voices as well as fair distribution of resources which provide the condition for equal participation. Fraser (1995), Young (1996; 1997 a/b) and Squires (1998) argue, with different emphases, that the unjust democratic exclusions of contemporary society are both cultural (the denial of recognition) and socio-economic (the inequality of distribution). The challenge for the era is to establish an understanding of justice which by embracing recognition (voice) and redistribution (resources), creates an inclusive society (or as Stewart (1999) argues, a just, inclusive democracy). Such a society will enable its citizens to develop the capabilities to acquire resources and to express themselves in the public sphere (cf. Martin et al., 1997; Martin and Vincent, 1999).

Understanding the Multi-voicedness of Learning Communities

A theory of learning has been developing over the past decade which places voice and dialogue at the centre of its pedagogy (Engestrom, 1995; Engestrom et al., 1999). Institutions in their contexts are analysed as socially and historically mediated 'activity systems' or 'communities of practice', which contain a variety of different viewpoints or 'voices', as well as layers of historically accumulated artefacts, rules and patterns of division of labour. The multivoiced and multilayered nature of activity systems can be a source of co-operation, but also of conflict and rivalry pointing to the need, if learning is to be effective, for procedures and traditions of conversation and dialogue, translation and negotiation. Of particular importance is the management of the boundaries of learning environments to enable learners to move coherently between settings. The challenge over time for a community of learners is to develop shared understanding and agreement—a common voice—about the learning process, its purposes, beliefs and activities. This shared system of meaning will need to be negotiated to enable mutual appropriation of ideas.

For Engestrom, the creating of a learning community takes place when its members learn to develop a third order of learning:

- learning as imitation or acquisition of conditioned responses;
- learning by doing, through problem solving or investigative learning to understand the deep-seated rules of a practice;
- learning to begin reflexively to question the existing community of practice and to learn how-to enter into a dialogue with others in order to transform practice, and in this way begin to design their own futures.

A number of 'learning cities' in Britain (Cara and Ranson, 1998; Cara et al., 1998)[2] believe that the key to regeneration lies in creating the conditions for such reflexive and dialogic learning communities to emerge: characterized by new forms of partnership between sectors and ways of listening to and involving the public. To avoid potential tension between these two strands, the partnerships need to become part of a broader public dialogue, the purpose of which is to clarify the future of the city, town or region in an era of global change. Traditionally, public services have been delivered to the public with too little consultation and involvement. Democracy has been at a distance from the communities which it was created to serve.

Now, many cities and towns are looking to find new ways of strengthening the important traditions of local democratic practice and understanding the contribution of participation to regeneration. This understanding has been learned in a number of European communities. Real learning communities will learn new kinds of engagements with their citizens to involve them in determining how their communities will be governed and changed. This process demands citizens who have the skills to articulate their needs and aspirations which are the same skills needed for work and leisure in a society which is in a state of change. The educational system has an important part to play in moving to such a culture of learning but other parts of the community—its democratic and cultural traditions—also have a key role to play in renewing the quality and vitality of public life.

Finding a Voice: the Core Capability

It is now clear that 'a new education' is emerging for a new age. During the past decade key research on learning has

[2] The concept of the learning city is relatively recent. It was promoted by an OECD/CERI study in 1992. This became a major influence on the development of the UK's Learning City Network which has grown steadily since 1996 to include more than 20 affiliated 'cities'. It is an important forum for debate on the potential of partnerships to link life-long learning with regeneration and local economic development. The meaning and purpose of a 'learning city' remain the subject of debate (cf. Landry and Mattarasso, 1998).

critically re-evaluated the dominant paradigm and proposed values and practices which amount to a new culture of learning (Gardner (1983), on multiple intelligence, Engestrom et al (1999) on learning communities, and Lave and Wenger (1990) on apprenticeship). Such research, however is not divorced from practice, as the leading reform programme of Professor Brighouse (1998) illustrates, or Tom Bentley's (1998) DEMOS study of active learning reveals, and is manifest in the work of government departments: the Scottish Office's prospectus on *new community education* (1998). This work proposes that education has traditionally been shaped by too narrow a conception of purpose, of human capacity, of frameworks of learning, and of assessment. The central principles informing the new pedagogy of capability for active citizenship:

- reconnect learning to living through preparation for active citizenship, enhancing the capacity for participation and dialogue;
- understand all the needs of the learner, particularly emotional well-being;
- enrich our understanding of human capability and potential: learners are able;
- promote active learning for developing responsible as well as reflective learners.

Taking a more holistic view of the learner and learning, means recognizing the central role which the family has at the centre of learning and the vital importance of encouraging relationships within families of mutual support for learning. Teachers have to break the tradition of keeping parents at a distance and learn to work in partnership with them.

Interviews with educators in the action zones reveal an emergent pedagogy of capability for inclusion and active citizenship. Learning, the argument proposes, depends upon motivation which grows out of a sense of purpose, of wanting to learn. This purpose is likely to be stimulated by the interests of the learner, but motivation which is likely to secure interest and to be enduring is when the learner, in wanting to do well, improve on their previous performance is self-motivated to learn more about the skills, qualities and virtues which lead to developing capability.

This growing awareness of purpose and of striving to improve one's capability and potential is, at the same time, a growing discovery of the self, of 'finding oneself', one's understanding about who I am, what I can do and what I am good at. This progress in accomplishment generates, but also presupposes, self understanding and self-respect. It is only when the learner experiences his or her particular identity being recognized, by and with others (cf. Ranson et al., 1996) that sense of an autonomous self with an awareness of its distinctive agency can unfold.

The challenge for educators is to make available to the learner the variety of experience which turns the stimulus of contingent interest into a deeper layer of being motivated to pursue the inner goods of capability and co-operative improvement. This understanding challenges the narrow instrumentality of much education policy about learning over the past two decades, which has neglected or subordinated the arts and cultural aspects of learning in favour of core skills which are believed to prepare young people directly for work. What are lost when these areas of learning experience are neglected are those vital dimensions of motivation for learning: the motivational conditions of acquiring the intrinsic goods of learning for the sake of capability and self-improvement:

Most importantly, developing a cultural dimension to learning takes learning away from being a purely instrumental purpose. It makes it personal learning, a development of the whole person. If learning is merely functional, you cut it off as soon as you have finished with it—because it is a banal experience. If however, we are learning for its own sake we want to learn it is something we enjoy, gain pleasure from and we enjoy getting better at, and want to develop ourselves because it is worthwhile. If the learning experience means something to you as a person, you will enjoy it, and take an interest in it, and continue to develop your skills because *you* want to improve your skills and standards of performance. You want to make yourself better, to improve. So by getting involved in sport and the arts and acquiring this motivation to learn to excel at something, they are learning to do well, to improve standards and this will carry over to other areas of their lives, and of course learning.

At the heart of this new pedagogy for active capability is understanding of the significance of 'finding a voice'—regarded as a vital means in learning to develop capability but also as embodying the purpose of learning to create confident young citizens able to contribute to the remaking of their communities. To learn to talk is to learn to:

- listen as well as express and communicate beliefs, feelings and claims
- enter a conversation with others which leads to
- develop(ing) understanding and reflection in contexts of different views
- discriminate and form judgements
- choose and decide for oneself and with others
- imagine and create a possible future

To find a voice is to find an identity and the possibility of agency in the world. Voice, the educators of the zones imply, is the inescapability capability which young people require to enter and flourish at the turn of the century. In a complex post-modern world of difference, the defining quality of citizenship will be the capability to find a voice which both asserts one's claims but also the need to enter a dialogue with others to reach shared understanding and agreement about how to resolve problems which are common to all in the public sphere (Nixon and Ranson, 1997; Ranson et al., 1999).

The Role of the Performance Arts in Empowering Voice

Educators in the EAZs understand the vital significance of core capabilities for disadvantaged young people. Literacy is regarded as crucial. Yet the literacy is conceived as more than an instrumental skill, however vital that is, and as providing the core communicative capability which empowers people to express their *voice* as citizens in the community:

We must significantly raise skills in the core areas. Reading, writing, listening etc, but the most important are communication, linguistic skills, these are the access to everything else. Without these core skills you struggle. The most important of the core skills is to be able to *talk*, to be articulate. Talk is so important (because it is the key to investigating and learning about new situations) we know when we are outside our comfort zone, when we don't understand the rituals of a new situation, we stay quiet; we listen, we watch. Then when we become accustomed, we begin to use our communication skills to develop understanding, and our confidence grows. So without these skills we couldn't move forward.

The implication of this understanding for learning and teaching is an urgent need to restore to the curriculum those activities which nourish self-esteem, confidence and voice, in particular the pedagogical significance of arts and culture:

One key challenge is to bring back into the curriculum the cultural aspects which have been neglected - music, art, sport. It is pedagogically vital because it is through culture that people understand about their life, their history and their past and therefore about their identities. They also gain pleasure from cultural activities, which also encourage talk. To understand you need a rich language. Getting involved in a specialist group - such as painting or music—will encourage language development. These interests will also provide opportunities for life-long learning. The achievements which come through participation in the arts or sport enhance a sense of success, stimulating motivation and they give pride to families who can see their youngsters achieving in activities.

The arts were one of those activities whose importance in the formative stages of learning was emphasised by the schools themselves and the local community. Children also learn through the expressive arts, and it was felt within the city that this was being neglected given the traditional focus within the national curriculum. Recognition of this led to setting up an Arts Forum.

The performance arts have a key role to play in developing the confidence, creative agency and motivation of learners:

> Drama, for example, is so important for learning because there are only you, the whole person that is the only thing that drama requires. You don't need prompts, it just needs you...In drama you work over a period of time and you work on trust and you work on how we are going to work together. Working with a group in drama you also establish a way of working together, how do we want to operate, how do we think we ought to behave towards each other? I do think you can negotiate with children—what do we want this room to be like? What do we want to happen here and then you get kids to say 'we don't want any put downs, we don't want to be sneered at'. And from this point you can go anywhere. You can release the imagination. And if you release the imagination, talk will develop and you create things and explore things which are happening to kids. (This can be a healing process) Kids draw on their experience and can start to make sense of it. The acting becomes a source for group discussion—talking about why she behaved like that; how else might she behave; was it inevitable that that happened? Its the questions I think that draw out of children perhaps a better understanding of what's

happening around them. I think they can perhaps make sense of what's happening around them together, and they can internalise it and they can start to see things aren't inevitable but there are choices. I think that's why its empowering, because drama is created by making a series of choices.

This zone is learning from research about the connection between singing and more traditional cognitive learning. The Director continued her analysis of the significance of the performance arts for learning:

I have got a link with *The Voices Foundation*. There work is based on the premise that everyone can learn to sing and sing well, and that non-specialists can teach singing to a high level. So they work in primary schools. But what their research has shown is that it has a knock on effect into intellectual development. Have you heard about assertive discipline? The teacher asks '*Are you listening*?' and the children reply '*We are listening*.' This may seem very trivial to you. But what they've discovered is that in cognitive abilities appear to have been enhanced through learning to sing and singing together. Because they have to listen, and listening is key to learning. Good singing is about finding the singing voice. We all have a singing voice which is different from the speaking voice. You start this with five year olds and work upwards. And in order to sing together well, you have to listen to others very well.

Underlying much of the discussion of learning has been the task of helping children to find a voice. Through voice children are enabled, empowered to assert their claims, express their feelings and thus contribute to conversations aiming at resolving the concerns which individuals, families and their communities confront. When young people and communities 'find a voice' they discover the first condition for discovering an agency that can challenge the constraint of alienating experience:

> Perhaps 'Finding a Voice' could be our slogan. We've signed up to the *Participation and Education Project*. It is run by a lady called Viv Schwartzburg, and has just had Lottery funding. It is based on a belief that children don't have a voice in schools, don't have a voice in terms of what is important to them. But schools have councils, school councils, which actually are terribly undemocratic. I think a lot of schools, I speak from experience, you set them up, but your not really into it. It should be about empowering children to have a voice. What PEP actually does is train young people, and train young people to train other young people to exercise their voice and so take responsibilities themselves.

Voice is important in the learning process, it is empowering, because it encourages young people in "learning to discriminate, judge, choose and so to improve their decision-making skills. Because otherwise learning is passive, and education shouldn't be passive ...' the empty vessel syndrome', haven't you? Fill them up with somebody else's information." This may have appeared to work for an earlier generation but in the information age of the internet, acquiring facts is not enough? "What is going to be increasingly important is that young people need to be discerning, need to be able to make judgements about the sheer volume of information that's going to be put in front of them. They need to be able to make decisions and, the older I get, the more I think life is about giving children decision-making skills, and actually seeing that, well if I do this, what might the consequences be."

These capabilities of voice and reflective deliberation will only emerge, it is argued, with the support of the appropriate institutional arrangements. These are beginning to emerge in some of the education action zones.

Dialogue with Family and Community

The pedagogy of new learning needs to be supported by institutional forms and patterns of governance which themselves embodies the educational values and purposes of inclusion, capability and active citizenship. The schools need to become 'learning schools', involving the different voices in a dialogue to develop shared understanding about institutional purpose and policy. Within this dialogue the participation and voice of the parents and the community are regarded as central: "we don't just articulate parental involvement as one of the six strands of policy—we see it as under-pinning all of the others as well":

> ... the big thing is that schools can't transform key skills, can't realise educational goals in isolation from families. Because the task is to do things differently, schools have to be on board for this agenda, and with parents involved in their children's education, with parents involved in the school. Schools need to become the base for family learning. We need to enhance family learning...

Schools are central to the development of the community. Schools need to be developed as study support centres, and as community college centres, which provide facilities six or seven days a week. Schools need to become a real resource for the community. This is important because in the past schools have closed ranks against the community. Schools have been precious, seeing education as their own preserve. But schools now need to be a community resource they are not the only educators.

The task for education is to cross the boundaries between school and the home, and the boundaries between education and other services. As Bentley (1999: 98)) puts it; 'Tackling underachievement, which begins with a focus on the individual learning, their motivation and strengths, as well as their weakness and barriers to success, depends on expanding outwards to include the whole learning environment, and the full richness of resources which it has to offer'. The more holistic view of the learner which the new education strives to achieve is reflected in the practice of focusing on the family unit to encourage and bring out the best in both parent and child through family learning and the development of positive parent child interaction (Alexander, 1997).

Some of the zones are encouraging schools to support the creation of family learning centres. Families are involved in running the centres and developing the facilities and activities which identify and support their learning needs. These centres also encourage self-help networks to grow (Bentley, 1999; Vincent and Warren, 1996).

In one rural zone, a family centre is being created in primary and secondary schools to support family learning in isolated communities. While in an inner city centre, a Family Support Strategy (FSS) has developed to provide better support for children and families through local partnerships which encourage statutory and voluntary agencies to work together more effectively. It is intended that local strategies will meet local needs, that services will be delivered when and where they are required, and that these will be properly co-ordinated from a local base. The voice of families from the different minority communities is increasingly heard in decision-making. The FSS has involved local families and community members in an audit of local needs and created an action plan. The central issue has been how to ensure services are more accessible to local people and that they are more effectively delivered.

Involving the Community

The policy initiative of EAZs has created them with a public Forum that is designed to constitute the principle of partnership and the opportunity for each of the partners to have a voice in regenerating education in the zone. "Our forum was set up in a way that expresses the broader partnerships that have been brought to bear upon education. There are still tensions actually: its a kind of platform for those interests to come into some kind of coherence or collision. Some heads find it difficult to meet with all the other interests around the table 'I am not sure that I like discussing education with all these other characters around the table. I am much more comfortable talking education here or within the cluster groups'." This Director, while depressed at this resistance, was not daunted believing it is right for the different interests, for example local businesses, to have a voice in clarifying purpose and policy within the zone.

For another zone, the challenge was more than constituting the forum as an expression of the partnership but one of constituting community governance, of the zone enabling the community to participate in the governance of the areas within which it lives and works. The perspective of this EAZ reflected their response to the perceived anger in the community but it also reflected a developing philosophy of public participation as the necessary value and purpose of a new local democracy.

The set up that we have put in place lately is the zone is very much an independent body from the LEA. We wanted to respond to the experience of community anger and so at a very early we wanted to get the community on board. In this, I think, we were at that time quite unique in terms of the zones throughout the country. We worked with the Resident's Association, which the housing department already had established. We also used the expertise within Youth and Community Services, again a different department of the Council, for their on-the-ground community workers. SRB, the year before, had also recognized a need for better links within the community and had employed community workers within quite a small area in terms of the overall zone.

This particular community was initially sceptical about EAZs, but wanted to be involved from the first so that they knew fully what was going on, and 'didn't feel that they were being spun any lines about all this money going into local areas, into the school'. They wanted to know exactly what the process was going to be. The community is well organized, through the residents and tenants associations, but while it has not been used to thinking about and getting organised around educational issues, they have taken the opportunity provided by the zone to voice their concerns about education as much as other services:

They were a valuable source of information just waiting to be asked. They were keen to express their views on educational issues without a doubt. They'd never had the forum. In terms of how the zone operates their voice is completely about education. They do not use that forum to raise other issues other than the work of the zone...They are there talking about educational issues and nothing else. You feel that they wanted to have a say, and if they had been given an opportunity in the past they would have had a say. Now they have the opportunity.

There has been a fundamental shift in terms of the way this Council interacts with the community, becoming committed to community participation, to consulting the public, and listening to the views it receives. It respects what the local population is saying at that point in time. There has been a change in culture. A number of mechanisms have been developed, including setting up citizens panels for consultation and they are creating focus groups on specific issues:

What are the communities saying about education? What is their voice? Basically what they are saying is that you can chuck as much money as you like at a school but if there is no regard for how well the school actually manages that money that will not necessarily ensure that every child is on level playing field and that all of the blocks of learning have been removed. What they are saying is through no fault of individuals they cannot access the same base levels for their children to actually be able to compete, and I don't mean that in the word to compete with others. So what they are saying is that the community is a massive resource, the parents are a massive resource who are generally not included in the way that they could be by schools. They wish to be recognised, there is a willingness to play a role supporting the learning of the their children and their community, because it isn't just about the kids in the school, its about life long learning aspects as well. The zone needs to be reflecting that and need to be really making sure that education is accessible to all.

Another zone in the north believes that the Authority's Community Councils have a role to play in closing the gap between the school and the community mean by listening to the voice of the community. They need to be improved by making them more representatives of the local communities. But there is a wealth of experience, of social capital, which can be drawn upon to support young people and their schools.

The zone needs to listen more to the young people, and the establishing of year group and whole school councils can encourage their voice to be expressed and heard. "There is one school where the governors set up the school council, and that were interesting because they listen to what the kids said.'

Towards Democratic Community Governance

The developing practices, within a number of zones, of valuing the inclusion of different voices in a learning community are part of more general emergent community governance. Designed to address traditional problems of disadvantage, social exclusion and underachievement, zones have been constituted as a new public partnership to create the social capital to transform the capabilities and achievement of communities facing entrenched disadvantage.

Traditionally, public services have been delivered to the public with limited consultation and involvement. Democracy was at a distance from the communities which it was created to serve. Neo-liberal thinking from the 1980's sought to fill the vacuum with a democracy of active consumers choosing public services amongst competing providers. For many localities, however this strategy was only reinforcing the problems of fragmentation and exclusion caused by the experience of global change (Gray; 1998; Luttwak, 1999). Many cities and towns have, therefore, begun to search for new ways of strengthening local democracy to make it more responsive to the changing needs of communities and to strive to involve them in the processes of economic and social regeneration. In this, a new citizenship of active participation in the governance of the community is emerging to counter and replace the traditions of client and consumer.

The leading theorist of community governance is John Stewart (1983; 1986; 1995; Stewart and Stoker, 1988; Ranson and Stewart, 1994; Clarke and Stewart, 1998). Early conceptions emphasiszd the changing role of the local authority from service provision to a strategic role in identifying the needs of the wider community through strengthened processes of local democracy. Some of the characteristics of community governance were perceived to include:

- 'the government of difference, both responding to differences in needs and aspirations and creating differences. One learns form difference rather than uniformity;
- a capacity for local choice, which creates the potential for innovation, and the learning made possible by that innovation;
- the diffusion of power-change is more easily made on the smaller scale, and there are limits to political capacity at the centre;
- a concern for the community beyond the mere provision of service;
- local and visible government-decisions can more easily involve when made close to the community than when made in corridors and committees of Central Government;

- a renewed basis for accountability in local democracy' (in Stewart and Stoker, 1988).

Now in a period of accelerating global change in the 1990s, communities need to learn new ways of governing themselves to secure this economic and democratic renewal: tackling exclusion by recognizing the different traditions, encouraging forms of active citizenship and participation to strengthen civil society. The emergent characteristics of new community governance are:

(*a*) Communities of difference and identity : We live increasingly within communities of difference. The post-modern world is typically characterised by clashes of cultural traditions whose values, histories and identities are said to be chronically agonistic and thus rival and incommensurable, compounded by a poverty of recognition and mutual understanding. Traditions shape 'critical points of deep and significant *difference* which constitute 'what we really are', or rather—since history has intervened—'what we have become' (Hall, 1990).

Many institutions and neighbourhoods within the community form a microcosm of the predicament facing the post-modern polity. The challenge for the new community governance is to discover processes which can reconcile the valuing of difference with the need for shared understanding and agreement about public purpose that dissolves prejudice and discrimination.

(*b*) Active citizenship : The motivation of members of society to acknowledge mutuality, to deliberate with others and to search for shared understanding is more likely to succeed if they regard each other as citizens with shared responsibility for collaborative making the communities in which they are to live (Ranson, 1997). This makes the *agency* of citizens central to personal and social development. Our active participation in creating the projects which are to shape our selves as well as the communities in which we live provides the sense of purpose to work together with others and to secure trusting relations with them. There is no solitary development or learning: we can only create our worlds together. The unfolding agency of the self always grows out of the interaction with others. It is *inescapably a social and creative making*. The self can only find its identity in and through others and membership of communities. The possibility of shared understanding requires individuals not only to value others but to create the communities in which mutuality and thus the conditions for learning can flourish.

The telos of citizenship is to learn to make the communities without which individuals and others cannot grow and develop. The presupposition of such making is *openness* to mutual recognition: we have to learn to be open to different perspectives, alternative life-forms and views of the world, to allow our pre-judgements to be challenged; in so doing we learn how to amend our assumptions, and develop an enriched understanding of others. The key to the transformation of prejudice lies in what Gadamer (1975) calls *'the dialogic character of understanding'*: through genuine conversation the participants are led beyond their initial positions, to take account of others, and move towards a richer, more comprehensive view, a 'fusion of horizons', a shared understanding of what is true or valid. Conversation lies at the heart of learning: they learn through dialogue to take a wider, more differentiated view, and thus acquire sensitivity, subtlety and capacity for judgement.

(*c*) Participation and voice for civil society : We can only make ourselves and our communities when empowered by a public domain which recognises the distinctively different contributions each have to give. For Habermas (1984), the processes of a discursive democracy provide the conditions for differences to be brought into the public sphere and negotiated through procedures of fair, equal and unconstrained discussion undistorted by power. Identities are respected and compromises, if not consensus, are reached between rival traditions.

Such a view of democracy recognises an understanding, effaced by rights based models, of the duality of citizenship: that citizens are both individuals and active members of the whole, the public as a political community. For Clarke (1996), this deep 'democratic citizenship' requires for the recovery of collaborative participation, the establishing and strengthening of the spaces, the intermediary institutions of civil society, in which such active citizenship can be practised (Keane, 1998; Hirst, 1994; Cohen and Rogers, 1995). A domain is formed in which private meets public, providing the conditions for what Mouffe argues strong democracy needs—an articulation between the particular and the universal. A sphere which recognises and mediates, through the arts of association, a diversity of particular interests for the public good. By providing forums for participation and voice the new polity can create the conditions for public discourse and for mutual accountability so that citizens can take each other's needs and claims into account will learn to create the conditions for each others development (Dunn, 1992).

(*d*) New institutional forms : *Stewart (1995; 1999),* in further developing his analysis of community governance has argued that if the public domain is to revitalize a citizenship for voice and dialogue, then institutional reform has to renew the institutional conditions for public life within communities leading to a new style of governing, linking the discourse of democracy and the government of collective choice. The conditions and lines of development include (Ranson and Stewart, 1994):

(*i*) An infrastructure of community forums—both of place and of interest—can provide the foundation to strengthen the constitutive principles of the public domain: enabling and expressing public discourse leading to collective choice based upon public consent.

(*ii*) Local government must be reconstituted as the community governing itself. It will have the responsibility for the development of community forums representing the diversity of communities within. As the expression of representative democracy it will set the framework for the development of participation through community forums and the means of discourse for reconciling difference and, if necessary, determining in collective choice. The upshot of such reform would be an institutional framework of community governance—with a capacity for integrating participative democracy and representative government—that can repair the vacuum of a polity the public legitimacy of which has withered.

(*iii*) Local government as the expression of the community governing itself, provides the systemic conditions for renewing the public domain. By establishing a framework of institutions, it enables the participation of citizens to be tied into the contribution of elected representatives in the forming of collective choice. In this way political capacity is enhanced, drawing together diversity of perspectives and values into a common process of discourse and decision that enhances the possibility of choice acquiring the authority of consent. Community governance thus provides the conditions for reconstruction, for what is demanded is a high capacity for learning both of the nature of the problems faced and about the approaches to adopt. The institutional arrangements of community governance enables citizens to participate and thus generate a more informed and responsive system of elected representation. It transforms representative democracy from a periodic event to a continuous process of representation. The interdependent complex of institutions provides the capacity for effective action monitored and evaluated by the public.'

A community, as Stewart (1999) argues, which learns to create institutional arrangements that include the variety of voices in its deliberations is likely to be a democratically just community and thus robust and capable enough to address the 'wicked collective action problems' which it faces at the turn of a new century.

REFERENCES

1. Alexander, T. (1997) *Family Learning: The Foundation of Effective Education*. London: Demos.
2. Austin, J.O. (1962) *How to do Things with Word.* Oxford: The Clarendon Press.
3. Barber, B. (1984) *Strong Democracy: Participatory Politics for a New Age.* Berkeley: University of California Press.
4. Bentley, T. (1998) *Learning Beyond the Classroom: Education for a Changing World.* London: Routledge.
5. Bentley, T. (1999) 'Family Learning', in *New Statesman* 19 March *Special Supplement, The Caring, Sharing Society* pp. xxvii.
6. Brighouse, T. and Woods, D. (1998) *How to Improve Your School.* London: Routledge.
7. Cara, S. and Ranson, S. (1998) *Practice, Progress and Value: Learning Communities: Assessing the Value they Add.* London: DfEE/Learning Cities Network.
8. Cara, S., Landry, C. and Ranson, S. (1998) *The Learning City for the Learning Age* Working Paper 10. London: Comedia in Association with Demos.
9. Castels, R. (1990) 'Extreme Cases of Marginalisation from Vulnerability to deaffiliation' reported in G. Room (ed) (1995) *Beyond the Threshold: The Measurement and Analysis of Social Exclusion.* Bristol: The Policy Press.
10. Clark, P. (1996) *Deep Citizenship.* London: Pluto.
11. Clarke, M. and Stewart, J. (1998) *Community Governance, Community Leadership and the new Local Government.* The University of Birmingham INLOGOV.
12. Cohen, J. and Rogers, J. (eds) (1995) *Associations and Democracy.* London: Verso.
13. Coole, D. (1996) Is Class a Difference that Makes a Difference? *Radical Philosophy,* 77: 17-25.
14. Duffy, K. (1995) *Social Exclusion and Human Dignity in Europe.* Strasbourg, Council of Europe.
15. Dunn, J. (1992) *Democracy.* Oxford: Oxford University Press.

16. Engestrom, R. (1995) 'Voice as Communicative Action', *Mind, Culture and Activity* 2(3): 192-215..
17. Engestrom, Y., Miettinen, R. and Punamaki, R. (1999) *Perspectives on Activity Theory* Cambridge, Cambridge University Press
18. Fraser, N. (1995) 'From Redistribution to Recognition? Dilemmas of Justice in a 'Post-socialist age, *New Left Review,* 212: 67-93.
19. Gadamer, H-G. (1975) *Truth and Method.* London: Sheed and Ward.
20. Gardner, H. (1983) *Frames of Mind.* London: Fontana.
21. Geddes, M. (1997) 'Poverty, Excluded Communities, and Local Democracy', in.
22. N. Jewson and S. Macgregor (eds) *Transforming Cities: Contested Governance and New Spatial Divisions.* London: Routledge pp.205-218.
23. Gray, J. (1998) *False Dawn: The Delusions of Global Capitalism.* London: Granta.
24. Hirst, P. (1994) *Associative Democracy.* Oxford: Polity.
25. Hirschmann, A. (1970) *Exit, Voice and Loyalty.* Cambridge: Harvard University Press.
26. Keane, J. (1988) *Democracy and Civil Society.* London: Verso.
27. Hall, S. (1990) 'Cultural Identity and Diaspora', in J. Rutherford (ed) *Identity, Community, Culture, Difference.* London: Lawrence and Wishart.
28. Lave, J. and Wenger, E. (1991) *Situated Learning: Legitimate Peripheral Participation.* Cambridge: Cambridge University Press.
29. Luttwak, E. (1999) *Turbo Capitalism: Winners and Losers in the Global Economy.* London: Orion.
30. Marshall, T. (1977) *Classes, Citizenship and Social Development.* Chicago: Chicago University Press.
31. Martin, J. (1996) School Based Empowerment: Giving Parents a Voice. *Local Government Policy Making* (Special Issue on Citizenship and Empowerment), 22(4): 18-24.
32. Martin, J. (1999) 'Social Justice, Education Policy and the Role of Parents: A Question of choice or voice', *Education and Social Justice,* 1 (2): 48-61.
33. Martin, J. (2000) 'Governing Institutions in Contexts of Cultural Diversity', in M. Leicester, C. Modgil and S. Modgil (eds) *Education,*

Culture and Values: Vol II Institutional Issues: Pupils, Schools and Teacher Education. London: Falmer.

34. Martin, J. and Vincent, C. (1999) 'Parental Voice: An Exploration' *International Journal in Sociology of Education,* 9 (2): 133-154.
35. Martin, J. Mckeown, P, Nixon, J and Ranson, S. (1997) 'School Governance for the Civil Society: Redefining the Boundary Between Schools and Parents', *Local Government Studies* 22 (4): 210-228.
36. Mingione, E. (1997) 'Enterprise and Exclusion, in Perri 6 (ed) *The Wealth and Poverty of Networks,* DEMOS Collection Issue 12, pp. 3-9.
37. Mouffe, C. (1993) *The Return of the Political.* London: Verso.
38. Mulgan, G. (1998) 'Social Exclusion: Joined Up Solutions to Joined Up Problems', in C. Oppenheim (ed) *An Inclusive Society: Strategies for Tackling Poverty* London, IPPR.
39. Nixon, J. and Ranson, S. (1997) 'Theorising 'Agreement': The Moral Bases of the Emergent Professionalism Within the New Management of Education *Discourse Studies in the Cultural Politics of Education,* 18 (2): 197-214.
40. Nussbaum, M. and Sen, A. (eds) (1994) *The Quality of Life.* Oxford,:The Clarenden Press.
41. Oppenheim, C. (ed) (1998) *An Inclusive Society: Strategies for Tackling Poverty* London, IPPR.
42. Parekh, B. (1988) Good Answers to Bad Questions *New Statesman and Society,* 28 October.
43. Perri 6 (1997) 'Social Exclusion: Time to be Optimistic', in Perri 6 (ed) *The Wealth and Poverty of Networks,* DEMOS Collection Issue12 pp. 3-9.
44. Phillips, A. (1995) *The Politics of Presence.* Oxford,: Oxford University Press.
45. Plant, R. (1990) Citizenship and Rights, in R. Plant and N. Barry (eds) *Citizenship and Rights in Thatcher's Britain: Two Views.* London: Institute of Economic Affairs.
46. Ranson, S. (1992) 'Towards the Learning Society', *Education Management and Administration* 20(1): 68-79.
47. Ranson, S. (1994) *Towards the Learning Society.* London: Cassell.
48. Ranson, S. (1997) 'For Citizenship and the Remaking of Civil Society', in R. Pring and G. Walford (eds) *Affirming the Comprehensive Ideal.* London: Falmer.

49. Ranson, S. (ed) (1998) *Inside the Learning Society.* London: Cassell.
50. Ranson, S. and Stewart, J. (1994) *Management for the Public Domain: Enabling the Learning Society*
51. Ranson, S, Martin, J, Mckeown, P. and Nixon, J. (1996) 'Towards a Theory of Learning' *British Journal of Educational Studies,* 44(1): 9-26.
52. Ranson, S., Martin, J., Mckeown, P. and Nixon, J. (1999) 'The New Management and Governance of Education', in G. Stoker (ed) *The New Management of British Local Governance.* London: Macmillan.
53. Room, G. (ed) (1995) *Beyond the Threshold: The Measurement and Analysis of Social Exclusion.* Bristol: The Policy Press.Rowntree, 1998
54. Sen, A. (1985) *Commodities and Capabilities.* Amsterdam: North-Holland.
55. Sen, A. (1990) 'Individual Freedom as a Social Commitment', *The New York Review* June 14 pp. 49-54
56. Silver, H. (1994) 'Social Exclusion and Social Solidarity: Three Paradigms', *International Labour Review,* 133(4-5): 531-558.
57. SOEID, (1998) *New Community Schools: The Prospectus.* Edinburgh: The Scottish Office.
58. Squires, J. (1998) 'In Different Voices: Deliberative Democracy and Aestheticist Politics', in J. Good and I. Velody (eds) *The Politics of Postmodernity.* Cambridge: Cambridge University Press.
59. Stewart, J. (1983) *Local Government: the Conditions of Local Choice.* London: George Allen and Unwin.
60. Stewart, J. (1986) *The New Management of Local Government.* London: Allen and Unwin.
61. Stewart, J. (1995) 'A Future for Local Government as Community Government', in J. Stewart and G. Stoker (eds) *Local Government in the 1990's.* London: Macmillan.
62. Stewart, J. (1999) 'Towards Democratic Justice', in *Local Routes to Social Justice*
63. Stewart, J. and Stoker, G. (1988) 'From Local Administration to Community Government', *Fabian Research Series* 351. London: Fabian Society.
64. Townsend, P. (1979) *Poverty in the United Kingdom.* Harmondsworth: Penguin.

65. Turner, B. (ed) (1993) *Citizenship and Social Theory.* London: Sage.

66. Vincent, C. (1996) *Parents and Teachers: Power and Participation.* London: Falmer.

67. Vincent, C. and Warren, S. (1998) Becoming a 'Better' Parent? Motherhood, Education and Transition *British Journal of Sociology of Education,* 19: 177-194.

68. Wertsch, J. (1991) *Voices of the Mind: A Socio-cultural Approach to Mediated Action.* Cambridge, Mass: Harvard University Press.

69. Yeatman, A. (1994) *Postmodern Revisionings of the Political.* London: Routledge.

70. Young, I. (1990) *Justice and the Politics of Difference.* Princeton: Princeton University Press.

71. Young, I. (1997) 'Identity *Vs.* Social Justice? *New Left Review* 222: 147-160.

72. Young, I. (1997) *Intersecting Voices: Dilemmas of Gender, Political Philosophy and Policy.* Princeton: Princeton University Press.

13

Theories of Educational Management

Tony Bush

SUMMARY

Educational management is a field of study and practice concerned with the operation of educational organizations. The present author has argued consistently (Bush, 1986; Bush, 1995; Bush, 1999; Bush, 2003) that educational management has to be centrally concerned with the purpose or aims of education. These purposes or goals provide the crucial sense of direction to underpin the management of educational institutions. Unless this link between purpose and management is clear and close, there is a danger of "managerialism . . . a stress on procedures at the expense of educational purpose and values" (Bush, 1999, p. 240). "Management possesses no super-ordinate goals or values of its own. The pursuit of efficiency may be the mission statement of management—but this is efficiency in the achievement of objectives which others define" (Newman and Clarke, 1994, p. 29).

NOTE

This module has been peer-reviewed, accepted, and sanctioned by the National Council of the Professors of Educational Administration (NCPEA) as a scholarly contribution to the knowledge base in educational administration.

The process of deciding on the aims of the organization is at the heart of educational management. In some settings, aims are decided by the principal, often working in association with senior colleagues and perhaps a small group of lay stakeholders. In many schools, however, goal setting is a corporate activity undertaken by formal bodies or informal groups.

School aims are strongly influenced by pressures from the external environment. Many countries have a national curriculum and these often leave little scope for schools to decide their own educational aims. Institutions may be left with the residual task of interpreting external imperatives rather than determining aims on the basis of their own assessment of student need. The key issue here is the extent to which school managers are able to modify government policy and develop alternative approaches based on school-level values and vision. Do they have to follow the script, or can they ad lib?

Distinguishing Educational Leadership and Management

The concept of management overlaps with two similar terms, leadership and administration. "Management" is widely used in Britain, Europe, and Africa, for example, while "administration" is preferred in the United States, Canada, and Australia. "Leadership" is of great contemporary interest in most countries in the developed World. Dimmock (1999) differentiates these concepts whilst also acknowledging that there are competing definitions:

School leaders [experience] tensions between competing elements of leadership, management and administration. Irrespective of how these terms are defined, school leaders experience difficulty in deciding the balance between higher order tasks designed to improve staff, student and school performance (leadership), routine maintenance of present operations (management) and lower order duties (administration). (p. 442)

Administration is not associated with "lower order duties" in the U.S. but may be seen as the overarching term, which embraces both leadership and management. Cuban (1988) provides one of the clearest distinctions between leadership and management. y leadership, I mean influencing others actions in achieving desirable ends...Managing is maintaining efficiently and effectively current organisational arrangements... . I prize both managing and leading and attach no special value to either since different settings and times call for varied responses. (p. xx)

Leadership and management need to be given equal prominence if schools are to operate effectively and achieve their objectives. "Leading and managing are distinct, but both are important.... The challenge of modern organisations requires the objective perspective of the manager as well as the flashes of vision and commitment-wise leadership provides" (Bolman and Deal, 1997, p. xiii-xiv).

The English National College for School Leadership

The contemporary emphasis on leadership rather than management is illustrated starkly by the opening of the English National College for School Leadership (NCSL) in November 2000. NCSL"s stress on leadership has led to a neglect of management. Visionary and inspirational leadership are advocated but much less attention is given to the structures and processes required to implement these ideas successfully. A fuller discussion of the NCSL may be found in Bush (2006).

The Significance of the Educational Context

Educational management as a field of study and practice was derived from management principles first applied to industry and commerce, mainly in the United States. Theory development largely involved the application of industrial models to educational settings. As the subject became established as an academic field in its own right, its theorists and practitioners began to develop alternative models based on their observation of, and experience in, schools and colleges. By the 21st century the main theories, featured in this chapter, have either been developed in the educational context or have been adapted from industrial models to meet the specific requirements of schools and colleges. Educational management has progressed from being a new field dependent upon ideas developed in other settings to become an established field with its own theories and research.

Conceptualising Educational Management

Leadership and management are often regarded as essentially practical activities. Practitioners and policy-makers tend to be dismissive of theories and concepts for their alleged remoteness from the "real" school situation. Willower (1980, p. 2), for example, asserts that "the application of theories by practicing administrators [is] a difficult and problematic undertaking. Indeed, it is clear that theories are simply not used very much in the realm of practice." This comment suggests that theory and practice are regarded as separate aspects of educational leadership and management. Academics develop and refine theory while managers engage in practice. In short, there is a theory/ practice divide, or "gap" (English, 2002):

> The theory-practice gap stands as the Gordian Knot of educational administration. Rather than be cut, it has become a permanent fixture of the landscape because it is embedded in the way we construct theories for use...The theory-practice gap will be removed when we construct different and better theories that predict the effects of practice. (p. 1, 3)

The Relevance of Theory to Good Practice

If practitioners shun theory then they must rely on experience as a guide to action. In deciding on their response to a problem they draw on a range of options suggested by previous experience with that type of issue. However, "it is wishful thinking to assume that experience alone will teach leaders everything they need to know" (Copland et al, 2002, p. 75).

Teachers sometimes explain their decisions as just "common sense." However, such apparently pragmatic decisions are often based on implicit theories. When a teacher or a manager takes a decision it reflects in part that person's view of the organization. Such views or preconceptions are coloured by experience and by the attitudes engendered by that experience. These attitudes take on the character of frames of reference or theories, which inevitably influence the decision-making process.

Theory serves to provide a rationale for decision-making. Managerial activity is enhanced by an explicit awareness of the theoretical framework underpinning practice in educational institutions. There are three main arguments to support the view that managers have much to learn from an appreciation of theory, providing that it is grounded firmly (Glaser and Strauss, 1967) in the realities of practice:

1. Reliance on facts as the sole guide to action is unsatisfactory because all evidence requires interpretation. Theory provides "mental models" (Leithwood et al, 1999, p. 75) to help in understanding the nature and effects of practice.

2. Dependence on personal experience in interpreting facts and making decisions is narrow because it discards the knowledge of others. Familiarity with the arguments and insights of theorists enables the practitioner to deploy a wide range of experience and understanding in resolving the problems of today. An understanding of theory also helps reduces the likelihood of mistakes occurring while experience is being acquired.

3. Experience may be particularly unhelpful as the sole guide to action when the practitioner begins to operate in a different context. Organizational variables may mean that practice in one school or college has little relevance in the new environment. A broader awareness of theory and practice may be valuable as the manager attempts to interpret behaviour in the fresh situation.

Of course, theory is useful only so long as it has relevance to practice in education. Hoyle (1986) distinguishes between theory-for-understanding and theory-for-practice. While both are potentially valuable, the latter is more significant for managers in education. The relevance of theory should be judged by the extent to which it informs managerial action and contributes to the resolution of practical problems in schools and colleges.

The Nature of Theory

There is no single all-embracing theory of educational management. In part this reflects the astonishing diversity of educational institutions, ranging from small rural elementary schools to very large universities and colleges. It relates also to the varied nature of the problems encountered in schools and colleges, which require different approaches and solutions. Above all, it reflects the multifaceted nature of theory in education and the social sciences: "Students of educational management who turn to organisational theory for guidance in their attempt to understand and manage educational institutions will not find a single, universally applicable theory but a multiplicity of theoretical approaches each jealously guarded by a particular epistemic community" (Ribbins, 1985, p. 223).

The existence of several different perspectives creates what Bolman and Deal (1997, p. 11) describe as "conceptual pluralism: a jangling discord of multiple voices." Each theory has something to offer in explaining behaviour and events in educational institutions. The perspectives favoured by managers, explicitly or implicitly, inevitably influence or determine decision-making.

Griffiths (1997) provides strong arguments to underpin his advocacy of "theoretical pluralism." "The basic idea is that all problems cannot be studied fruitfully using a single theory. Some problems are large and complex and no single theory is capable of encompassing them, while others, although seemingly simple and straightforward, can be better understood through the use of multiple theories . . . particular theories are appropriate to certain problems, but not others" (Griffiths, 1997, p. 372).

The Characteristics of Theory

Most theories of educational leadership and management possess three major characteristics:

1. Theories tend to be normative in that they reflect beliefs about the nature of educational institutions and the behaviour of individuals within them. Simkins (1999) stresses the importance of distinguishing between descriptive and normative uses of theory. "This is a distinction which is often not clearly made. The former are those which attempt to describe the nature of organisations and how they work and, sometimes, to explain why they are as they are. The latter, in contrast, attempt to prescribe how organisations should or might be managed to achieve particular outcomes more effectively" (p. 270).
2. Theories tend to be selective or partial in that they emphasize certain aspects of the institution at the expense of other elements. The espousal of one theoretical model leads to the neglect of other approaches. Schools and colleges are arguably too complex to be capable of analysis through a single dimension.
3. Theories of educational management are often based on, or supported by, observation of practice in educational institutions. English (2002, p. 1) says that observation may be used in two ways. First,

observation may be followed by the development of concepts, which then become theoretical frames. Such perspectives based on data from systematic observation are sometimes called "grounded theory." Because such approaches are derived from empirical inquiry in schools and colleges, they are more likely to be perceived as relevant by practitioners. Secondly, researchers may use a specific theoretical frame to select concepts to be tested through observation. The research is then used to "prove" or "verify" the efficacy of the theory (English, 2002, p. 1).

Models of Educational Management: An Introduction

Several writers have chosen to present theories in distinct groups or bundles but they differ in the models chosen, the emphasis given to particular approaches and the terminology used to describe them. Two of the best known frameworks are those by Bolman and Deal (1997) and Morgan (1997).

In this chapter, the main theories are classified into six major models of educational management (Bush, 2003). All these models are given significant attention in the literature of educational management and have been subject to a degree of empirical verification. Fig. 13.1 shows the six models and links them to parallel leadership models. The links between management and leadership models are given extended treatment in Bush (2003).

Management model	Leadership model
Formal	Managerial
Collegial	Participative
Political	Transactional
Subjective	Post-modem
Ambiguity	Contingency
Cultural	Moral

Fig. 13.1. Typology of management and leadership models (adopted from Bush and Glover 2002)

Formal Models

Formal model is an umbrella term used to embrace a number of similar but not identical approaches. The title "formal" is used because these theories emphasize the official and structural elements of organizations:

Formal models assume that organisations are hierarchical systems in which managers use rational means to pursue agreed goals. Heads possess authority legitimised by their formal positions within the organisation and are accountable to sponsoring bodies for the activities of their organisation (Bush, 2003, p. 37).

This model has seven major features:

1. They tend to treat organizations as systems. A system comprises elements that have clear organisational links with each other. Within schools, for example, departments and other sub-units are systemically related to each other and to the institution itself.
2. Formal models give prominence to the official structure of the organization. Formal structures are often represented by organization charts, which show the authorized pattern of relationships between members of the institution.
3. In formal models the official structures of the organization tend to be hierarchical. Teachers are responsible to department chairs that, in turn, are answerable to principals for the activities of their departments. The hierarchy thus represents a means of control for leaders over their staff.
4. All formal approaches typify schools as goal-seeking organizations. The institution is thought to have official purposes, which are accepted and pursued by members of the organization. Increasingly, goals are set within a broader vision of a preferred future for the school (Beare, Caldwell, and Millikan, 1989).

5. Formal models assume that managerial decisions are made through a rational process. Typically, all the options are considered and evaluated in terms of the goals of the organization. The most suitable alternative is then selected to enable those objectives to be pursued.
6. Formal approaches present the authority of leaders as a product of their official positions within the organization. Principals" power is positional and is sustained only while they continue to hold their posts.

In formal models there is an emphasis on the accountability of the organization to its sponsoring body. Most schools remain responsible to the school district. In many centralised systems, school principals are accountable to national or state governments. In decentralised systems, principals are answerable to their governing boards.

(Adapted from Bush, 2003, p. 37-38).

These seven basic features are present to a greater or lesser degree in each of the individual theories, which together comprise the formal models. These are:

- structural models;
- systems models;
- bureaucratic models;
- rational models;
- hierarchical models.

A full discussion of each of these sub-models appears in Bush (2003).

Managerial Leadership

The type of leadership most closely associated with formal models is "managerial." Managerial leadership assumes that the focus of leaders ought to be on functions, tasks and behaviours and that if these functions are carried out competently the work of others in the organisation will be facilitated. Most approaches to managerial leadership also assume that the behaviour of organisational members is largely rational. Authority and influence are allocated to formal positions in proportion to the status of those positions in the organisational hierarchy. (Leithwood et al, 1999, p. 14)

Dressler's (2001) review of leadership in Charter schools in the United States shows the significance of managerial leadership: "Traditionally, the principal"s role has been clearly focussed on management responsibilities" (p. 175). Managerial leadership is focused on managing existing activities successfully rather than visioning a better future for the school.

The Limitations of Formal Models

The various formal models pervade much of the literature on educational management.

They are normative approaches in that they present ideas about how people in organizations ought to behave. Levacic et al (1999) argue that these assumptions underpin the educational reforms of the 1990s, notably in England:

A major development in educational management in the last decade has been much greater emphasis on defining effective leadership by individuals in management posts in terms of the effectiveness of their organisation, which is increasingly judged in relation to measurable outcomes for students . . . This is argued to require a rational-technicist approach to the structuring of decision-making. (p. 15)

There are five specific weaknesses associated with formal models:

1. It may be unrealistic to characterize schools and colleges as goal-oriented organizations. It is often difficult to ascertain the goals of educational institutions. Formal objectives may have little operational relevance because they are often vague

and general, because there may be many different goals competing for resources, and because goals may emanate from individuals and groups as well as from the leaders of the organisation.

Even where the purposes of schools and colleges have been clarified, there are further problems in judging whether objectives have been achieved. Policy-makers and practitioners often rely on examination performance to assess schools but this is only one dimension of the educational process.

2. The portrayal of decision-making as a rational process is fraught with difficulties. The belief that managerial action is preceded by a process of evaluation of alternatives and a considered choice of the most appropriate option is rarely substantiated. Much human behaviour is irrational and this inevitably influences the nature of decision-making in education. Weick (1976, p. 1), for example, asserts that rational practice is the exception rather than the norm.

3. Formal models focus on the organization as an entity and ignore or underestimate the contribution of individuals. They assume that people occupy preordained positions in the structure and that their behaviour reflects their organizational positions rather than their individual qualities and experience. Greenfield (1973)has been particularly critical of this view (see the discussion of subjective models, below). Samier (2002, p. 40) adopts a similar approach, expressing concern "about the role technical rationality plays in crippling the personality of the bureaucrat, reducing him [sic] to a cog in a machine."

4. A central assumption of formal models is that power resides at the apex of the pyramid. Principals possess authority by virtue of their positions as the appointed leaders of their institutions. This focus on official

authority leads to a view of institutional management which is essentially top down. Policy is laid down by senior managers and implemented by staff lower down the hierarchy. Their acceptance of managerial decisions is regarded as unproblematic.

Organizations with large numbers of professional staff tend to exhibit signs of tension between the conflicting demands of professionalism and the hierarchy. Formal models assume that leaders, because they are appointed on merit, have the competence to issue appropriate instructions to subordinates. Professional organizations have a different ethos with expertise distributed widely within the institution. This may come into conflict with professional authority.

5. Formal approaches are based on the implicit assumption that organizations are relatively stable. Individuals may come and go but they slot into predetermined positions in a static structure. "Organisations operating in simpler and more stable environments are likely to employ less complex and more centralised structures, with authority, rules and policies as the primary vehicles for co-ordinating the work" (Bolman and Deal, 1997, p. 77).

Assumptions of stability are unrealistic in contemporary schools. March and Olsen (1976, p.21) are right to claim that "Individuals find themselves in a more complex, less stable and less understood world than that described by standard theories of organisational choice."

Are Formal Models Still Valid?

These criticisms of formal models suggest that they have serious limitations. The dominance of the hierarchy is compromised by the expertise possessed by professional staff. The supposed rationality of the decision-making process requires modification to allow for the pace and complexity of change. The concept of organizational goals is challenged by those who point to the existence of multiple objectives in education and the possible conflict between goals held at individual, departmental and institutional levels. "Rationalistic-bureaucratic notions...have largely proven to be sterile and to have little application to administrative practice in the "real world" (Owens & Shakeshaft,1992,p. 4)

Despite these limitations, it would be inappropriate to dismiss formal approaches as irrelevant to schools and colleges. The other models discussed in this chapter were all developed as a reaction to the perceived weaknesses of formal theories. However, these alternative perspectives have not succeeded in dislodging the formal models, which remain valid as partial descriptions of organization and management in education. Owens and Shakeshaft (1992)refer to a reduction of confidence in bureaucratic models, and a "paradigm shift" to a more sophisticated analysis, but formal models still have much to contribute to our understanding of schools as organisations.

COLLEGIAL MODELS

Central Features of Collegial Models

Collegial models include all those theories that emphasize that power and decision-making should be shared among some or all members of the organization (Bush, 2003):

Collegial models assume that organizations determine policy and make decisions through a process of discussion leading to consensus. Power is shared among some or all members of the organization who are thought to have a shared understanding about the aims of the institution. (p. 64)

Brundrett (1998) says that "collegiality can broadly be defined as teachers conferring and collaborating with other teachers" (p. 305). Little (1990) explains that "the reason to pursue the study and practice of collegiality is that, presumably, something is gained when teachers work together and something is lost when they do not" (p. 166).

Collegial models have the following major features:

1. They are strongly normative in orientation. "The advocacy of collegiality is made more on the basis of prescription than on research-based studies of school practice" (Webb and Vulliamy, 1996, p. 443).
2. Collegial models seem to be particularly appropriate for organizations such as schools and colleges that have significant numbers of professional staff. Teachers have an authority of expertise that contrasts with the positional authority associated with formal models. Teachers require a measure of autonomy in the classroom but also need to collaborate to ensure a coherent approach to teaching and learning (Brundrett, 1998, p. 307). Collegial models assume that professionals also have a right to share in the wider decision-making process. Shared decisions are likely to be better informed and are also much more likely to be implemented effectively.
3. Collegial models assume a common set of values held by members of the organization. These common values guide the managerial activities of the organization and are thought to lead to shared educational objectives. The common values of professionals form part of the justification for the optimistic assumption that it is always possible to reach agreement about goals and policies. Brundrett (1998, p. 308) goes further in referring to the importance of "shared vision" as a basis for collegial decision-making.
4. The size of decision-making groups is an important element in collegial management. They have to be sufficiently small to enable everyone to be heard. This may mean that collegiality works better in elementary schools, or in sub-units, than at the institutional level in secondary schools. Meetings of the whole staff may operate collegially in small schools but may be suitable only for information exchange in larger institutions.

The collegial model deals with this problem of scale by building-in the assumption that teachers have formal representation within the various decision-making bodies. The democratic element of formal representation rests on the allegiance owed by participants to their constituencies (Bush, 2003, p. 67).

5. Collegial models assume that decisions are reached by consensus. The belief that there are common values and shared objectives leads to the view that it is both desirable and possible to resolve problems by agreement. The decision-making process may be elongated by the search for compromise but this is regarded as an acceptable price to pay to maintain the aura of shared values and beliefs. The case for consensual decision-making rests in part on the ethical dimension of collegiality. Imposing decisions on staff is considered morally repugnant, and inconsistent with the notion of consent.(Bush, 2003, p. 65-67).

Participative Leadership

Because policy is determined within a participative framework, the principal is expected to adopt participative leadership strategies. Heroic models of leadership are inappropriate when influence and power are widely distributed within the institution. "The collegial leader is at most a "first among equals" in an academic organisation supposedly run by professional experts...the collegial leader is not so much a star standing alone as the developer of consensus among the professionals who must share the burden of the decision." (Baldridge et al, 1978, p. 45)

While transformational leadership is consistent with the collegial model, in that it assumes that leaders and staff have shared values and common interests (Bush, 2003, p. 76), the leadership model most relevant to collegiality is "participative leadership," which "assumes that the decision-making processes of the group ought to be the central focus of the group" (Leithwood et al, 1999, p. 12). This is a normative model, underpinned by three criteria (Leithwood et al., 1999):

- Participation will increase school effectiveness.
- Participation is justified by democratic principles.
- Leadership is potentially available to any legitimate stakeholder. (p. 12)

Sergiovanni (1984) claims that a participative approach succeeds in "bonding" staff together and in easing the pressures on school principals. "The burdens of leadership will be less if leadership functions and roles are shared and if the concept of leadership density were to emerge as a viable replacement for principal leadership" (p. 13).

Limitations of Collegial Models

Collegial models have been popular in the academic and official literature on educational collegial models has been popular in the academic and official literature on educational management since the 1980s. However, their critics point to a number of limitations:

Collegial models are so strongly normative that they tend to obscure rather than portray reality. Precepts about the most appropriate ways of managing educational institutions mingle with descriptions of behaviour. While collegiality is increasingly advocated, the evidence of its presence in schools and colleges tends to be sketchy and incomplete. "The collegial literature often confuses descriptive and normative enterprises.

The collegial idea of round table decision making does not accurately reflect the actual processes in most institutions" (Baldridge et al, 1978, p. 33).

2. Collegial approaches to decision-making tend to be slow and cumbersome. When policy proposals require the approval of a series of committees, the process is often tortuous and time consuming. Participants may have to endure many

lengthy meetings before issues are resolved. This requires patience and a considerable investment of time. Several English primary school heads interviewed by Webb and Vulliamy (1996) refer to the time-consuming nature of meetings where "the discussion phase seemed to go on and on" (p. 445) and "I felt we weren't getting anywhere" (p. 446).

3. A fundamental assumption of democratic models is that decisions are reached by consensus. It is believed that the outcome of debate should be agreement based on the shared values of participants. In practice, though, teachers have their own views and may also represent constituencies within the school or college. Inevitably these sectional interests have a significant influence on committees' processes. The participatory framework may become the focal point for disagreement between factions.

4. Collegial models have to be evaluated in relation to the special features of educational institutions. The participative aspects of decision-making exist alongside the structural and bureaucratic components of schools and colleges. Often there is tension between these rather different modes of management. The participative element rests on the authority of expertise possessed by professional staff but this rarely trumps the positional authority of official leaders or the formal power of external bodies. Brundrett (1998) claims that "collegiality is inevitably the handmaiden of an ever increasingly centralised bureaucracy" (p. 313)

5. Collegial approaches to school and college decision-making may be difficult to sustain because principals remain accountable to various external groups. They may experience considerable difficulty in defending policies that have emerged from a collegial process but do not enjoy their personal support. Brundrett (1998) is right to argue that "heads need to be genuinely brave to lend power to a democratic forum which may make decisions with which the headteacher may not themselves agree" (p. 310).

6. The effectiveness of a collegial system depends in part on the attitudes of staff. If they actively support participation then it may succeed. If they display apathy or hostility, it seems certain to fail. Wallace (1989) argues that teachers may not welcome collegiality because they are disinclined to accept any authority intermediate between themselves and the principal.

7. Collegial processes in schools depend even more on the attitudes of principals than on the support of teachers. Participative machinery can be established only with the support of the principal, who has the legal authority to manage the school. Hoyle (1986) concludes that its dependence on the principal's support limits the validity of the collegiality model.

Contrived Collegiality

Hargreaves (1994) makes a more fundamental criticism of collegiality, arguing that it is being espoused or "contrived" by official groups in order to secure the implementation of national or state policy. Contrived collegiality has the following features (Hargreaves, 1994):

- Administratively regulated rather than spontaneous.
- Compulsory rather than discretionary.
- Geared to the implementation of the mandates of government or the principal.
- Fixed in time and place.
- Designed to have predictable outcomes. (p. 195-196)

Webb and Vulliamy (1996) argue that collegial frameworks may be used for essentially political activity, the focus of the next section of this chapter (Webb and Vulliamy, 1996):

> The current climate...encourages headteachers to be powerful and, if necessary, manipulative leaders in order to ensure that policies and practices agreed upon are ones that they can wholeheartedly support and defend. (p. 448)

Is Collegiality an Unattainable Ideal?

Collegial models contribute several important concepts to the theory of educational management. Participative approaches are a necessary antidote to the rigid hierarchical assumptions of the formal models. However, collegial perspectives underestimate the official authority of the principal and present bland assumptions of consensus, which often cannot be substantiated. Little (1990) following substantial research in the United States, concludes that collegiality "turns out to be rare" (p.187). Collegiality is an elusive ideal but a measure of participation is essential if schools are to be harmonious and creative organisations.

POLITICAL MODELS

Central Features of Political Models

Political models embrace those theories that characterize decision-making as a bargaining process. Analysis focuses on the distribution of power and influence in organizations and on the bargaining and negotiation between interest groups. Conflict is regarded as endemic within organizations and management is directed towards the regulation of political behaviour (Bush, 2003):

Political models assume that in organizations policy and decisions emerge through a process of negotiation and bargaining. Interest groups develop and form alliances in pursuit of particular policy objectives. Conflict is viewed as a natural phenomenon and power accrues to dominant coalitions rather than being the preserve of formal leaders. (p. 89)

Baldridge's (1971) research in universities in the U.S. led him to conclude that the political model, rather than the formal or collegial perspectives, best captured the realities of life in higher education.

Political models have the following major features:

1. They tend to focus on group activity rather than the institution as a whole. Ball (1987) refers to "baronial politics" (p. 221) and discusses the nature of conflict between the leaders of subgroups. He adds that conflict between "barons" is primarily about resources and power.
2. Political models are concerned with interests and interest groups. Individuals are thought to have a variety of interests that they pursue within the organization. In talking about "interests," we are talking about pre-dispositions embracing goals, values, desires, expectations, and other orientations and inclinations that lead a person to act in one way rather than another (Morgan, 1997, p. 61).
3. Political models stress the prevalence of conflict in organizations. Interest groups pursue their independent objectives, which may contrast sharply with the aims of other subunits within the institution and lead to conflict between them. "Conflict will always be present in organisations...its source rests in some perceived or real divergence of interests" (Morgan, 1997, p. 167).
4. Political models assume that the goals of organizations are unstable, ambiguous and contested. Individuals, interest groups and coalitions have their own purposes and act towards their achievement. Goals may be disputed and then become a significant element in the conflict between groups (Bolman and Deal, 1991):

The political frame...insists that organisational goals are set through negotiations among the members of coalitions. Different individuals and groups have different objectives and resources, and each attempt to bargain with other members or coalitions to influence goals and decision-making process. (p. 190)

5. As noted above, decisions within political arenas emerge after a complex process of bargaining and negotiation. "Organisational goals and decisions emerge from ongoing processes of bargaining, negotiation, and jockeying for position among members of different coalitions" (Bolman and Deal, 1991, p. 186).
6. The concept of power is central to all political theories. The outcomes of the complex decision-making process are likely to be determined according to the relative power of the individuals and interest groups involved in the debate. "Power is the medium through which conflicts of interest are ultimately resolved. Power influences who gets what, when and how...the sources of power are rich and varied" (Morgan, 1997, p. 170-171).

Sources of Power in Education

Power may be regarded as the ability to determine the behaviour of others or to decide the outcome of conflict. Where there is disagreement it is likely to be resolved according to the relative resources of power available to the participants. There are many sources of power but in broad terms a distinction can be made between authority and influence. Authority is legitimate power, which is vested in leaders within formal organizations. Influence depends on personal characteristics and expertise.

There are six significant forms of power relevant to schools and colleges:

1. *Positional Power :* A major source of power in any organization is that accruing to individuals who hold an official position in the institution. Handy (1993, p. 128) says that positional power is "legal" or "legitimate" power. In schools, the principal is regarded as the legitimate leader and possesses legal authority.

2. *Authority of Expertise :* In professional organizations there is a significant reservoir of power available to those who possess appropriate expertise. Teachers, for example, have specialist knowledge of aspects of the curriculum. "The expert...often carries an aura of authority and power that can add considerable weight to a decision that rests in the balance" (Morgan, 1997, p. 181).
3. *Personal Power :* Individuals who are charismatic or possess verbal skills or certain other characteristics may be able to exercise personal power. These personal skills are independent of the power accruing to individuals by virtue of their position in the organization (Bolman and Deal, 1991).
4. *Control of Rewards :* Power is likely to be possessed to a significant degree by individuals who have control of rewards. In education, rewards may include promotion, good references, and allocation to favoured classes or groups. Individuals who control or influence the allocation of these benefits may be able to determine the behaviour of teachers who seek one or more of the rewards.
5. *Coercive Power :* The mirror image of the control of rewards may be coercive power. This implies the ability to enforce compliance, backed by the threat of sanctions. "Coercive power rests on the ability to constrain, to block, to interfere, or to punish" (Bolman and Deal, 1991, p. 196).

Control of Resources

Control of the distribution of resources may be an important source of power in educational institutions, particularly in self-managing schools. Decisions about the allocation of resources are likely to be among the most significant aspects of the policy process in such organisations. Control of these resources may give power over those people who wish to acquire them.

Consideration of all these sources of power leads to the conclusion that principals possess substantial resources of authority and influence. However, they do not have absolute power. Other leaders and teachers also have power, arising principally from their personal qualities and expertise. These other sources of power may act as a counter-balance to the principal's positional authority and control of rewards.

Transactional Leadership

The leadership model most closely aligned with political models is that of transactional leadership. "Transactional leadership is leadership in which relationships with teachers are based upon an exchange for some valued resource. To the teacher, interaction between administrators and teachers is usually episodic, short-lived and limited to the exchange transaction" (Miller and Miller, 2001, p. 182).

This exchange process is an established political strategy. As we noted earlier, principals hold power in the form of key rewards such as promotion and references. However, they require the co-operation of staff to secure the effective management of the school. An exchange may secure benefits for both parties to the arrangement. The major limitation of such a process is that it does not engage staff beyond the immediate gains arising from the transaction. Transactional leadership does not produce long-term commitment to the values and vision promoted by school leaders.

The Limitations of Political Models

Political models are primarily descriptive and analytical. The focus on interests, conflict between groups, and power provides a valid and persuasive interpretation of the decision-making process in schools. However, these theories do have four major limitations:

1. Political models are immersed so strongly in the language of power, conflict and manipulation that they neglect other standard aspects of organizations. There is little recognition that most organizations operate for much of the time according to routine bureaucratic procedures. The focus is heavily on policy formulation while the implementation of policy receives little attention. The outcomes of bargaining and negotiation are endorsed, or may falter, within the formal authority structure of the school or college.
2. Political models stress the influence of interest groups on decision-making. The assumption is that organizations are fragmented into groups, which pursue their own independent goals. This aspect of political models may be inappropriate for elementary schools, which may not have the apparatus for political activity. The institutional level may be the center of attention for staff in these schools, invalidating the political model's emphasis on interest group fragmentation.
3. In political models there is too much emphasis on conflict and a neglect of the possibility of professional collaboration leading to agreed outcomes. The assumption that teachers are engaged in a calculated pursuit of their own interests underestimates the capacity of teachers to work in harmony with colleagues for the benefit of their pupils and students.
4. Political models are regarded primarily as descriptive or explanatory theories. Their advocates claim that these approaches are realistic portrayals of the decision-making process in schools and colleges. There is no suggestion that teachers should pursue their own self-interest, simply an assessment, based on observation, that their behaviour is consistent with apolitical perspective. Nevertheless, the less attractive aspects of political models may make them unacceptable to many educationists for ethical reasons.

Are Political Models Valid?

Political models provide rich descriptions and persuasive analysis of events and behaviour in schools and colleges. The explicit recognition of interests as prime motivators for action is valid, as are the concepts of conflict and power. For many teachers and school leaders, political models fit their experience of day-to-day reality in schools. Lindle (1999), a school administrator in the United States, argues that it is a pervasive feature of schools.

SUBJECTIVE MODELS

Central Features of Subjective Models

Subjective models focus on individuals within organizations rather than the total institution or its subunits. These perspectives suggest that each person has a subjective and selective perception of the organization. Events and situations have different meanings for the various participants in institutions. Organizations are portrayed as complex units, which reflect the numerous meanings and perceptions of all the people within them. Organizations are social constructions in the sense that they emerge from the interaction of their participants. They are manifestations of the values and beliefs of individuals rather than the concrete realities presented in formal models (Bush, 2003):

Subjective models assume that organizations are the creations of the people within them. Participants are thought to interpret situations in different ways and these individual perceptions are derived from their background and values. Organizations have different meanings for each of their members and exist only in the experience of those members. (p. 113)

Subjective models became prominent in educational management as a result of the work of Thomas Greenfield in the 1970s and 1980s. Greenfield was concerned about several aspects of systems theory, which he regarded as the dominant model of educational organizations. He argues that systems theory is "bad theory" and criticizes its focus on the institution as a concrete reality (Greenfield, 1973):

> Most theories of organisation grossly simplify the nature of the reality with which they deal. The drive to see the organisation as a single kind of entity with a life of its own apart from the perceptions and beliefs of those involved in it blinds us to its complexity and the variety of organisations people create around themselves. (p. 571)

Subjective models have the following major features:

They focus on the beliefs and perceptions of individual members of organizations rather than the institutional level or interest groups. The focus on individuals rather than the organization is a fundamental difference between subjective and formal models, and creates what Hodgkinson (1993) regards as an unbridgeable divide. "A fact can never entail a value, and an individual can never become a collective" (p. xii).

Subjective models are concerned with the meanings placed on events by people within organizations. The focus is on the individual interpretation of behaviour rather than the situations and actions themselves. "Events and meanings are loosely coupled: the same events can have very different meanings for different people because of differences in the schema that they use to interpret their experience" (Bolman and Deal, 1991, p. 244).

The different meanings placed on situations by the various participants are products of their values, background and experience. So the interpretation of events depends on the beliefs held by each member of the organization. Greenfield (1979) asserts that formal theories make the mistake of treating the meanings of leaders as if they were the objective realities of the organization. "Too frequently in the past, organisation and administrative theory has... taken sides in the ideological battles of social process and presented as 'theory'" (p. 103) , the views of a dominating set of values, the views of rulers, elites, and their administrators.

Subjective models treat structure as a product of human interaction rather than something that is fixed or predetermined. The organization charts, which are characteristic of formal models, are regarded as fictions in that they cannot predict the behaviour of individuals. Subjective approaches move the emphasis away from structure towards a consideration of behaviour and process. Individual behaviour is thought to reflect the personal qualities and aspirations of the participants rather than the formal roles they occupy. "Organisations exist to serve human needs, rather than the reverse" (Bolman & Deal, 1991, p. 121).

Subjective approaches emphasize the significance of individual purposes and deny the existence of organizational goals. Greenfield (1973) asks "What is an organisation that it can have such a thing as a goal?" (p. 553). The view that organizations are simply the product of the interaction of their members leads naturally to the assumption that objectives are individual, not organizational (Bush, 2003, p. 114-118).

Subjective Models and Qualitative Research

The theoretical dialectic between formal and subjective models is reflected in the debate about positivism and interpretive in educational research. Subjective models relate to a mode of research that is predominantly interpretive or qualitative. This approach to enquiry is based on the subjective experience of individuals. The main aim is to seek understanding of the ways in which individuals create, modify and interpret the social world which they inhabit.

The main features of interpretive, or qualitative, research echo those of the subjective models:

1. They focus on the perceptions of individuals rather than the whole organisation. The subject's individual

perspective is central to qualitative research (Morrison, 2002, p. 19).

2. Interpretive research is concerned with the meanings, or interpretations, placed on events by participants. "All human life is experienced and constructed from a subjective perspective" (Morrison, 2002, p. 19).
3. Research findings are interpreted using "grounded" theory. "Theory is emergent and must arise from particular situations; it should be "grounded" on data generated by the research act. Theory should not proceed research but follow it" (Cohen et al, 2000, p. 23).

Post-modern Leadership

Subjective theorists prefer to stress the personal qualities of individuals rather than their official positions in the organization. The subjective view is that leadership is a product of personal qualities and skills and not simply an automatic outcome of official authority.

The notion of post-modern leadership aligns closely with the principles of subjective models. Keough and Tobin (2001, p. 2) say that "current post-modern culture celebrates the multiplicity of subjective truths as defined by experience and revels in the loss of absolute authority." They identify several key features of post-modernism (Keough and Tobin, 2001):

Language does not Reflect Reality

- Reality does not exist; there are multiple realities.
- Any situation is open to multiple interpretations.
- Situations must be understood at local level with particular attention to diversity.

Sackney and Mitchell (2001) stress the centrality of individual interpretation of events while also criticising visionary leadership. "Leaders must pay attention to the cultural and symbolic structure of meaning construed by individuals and groups...post-modern theories of leadership take the focus off vision and place it squarely on voice" (p. 13-14). Instead of a compelling vision articulated by leaders, there are multiple voices, and diverse cultural meanings.

The Limitations of Subjective Models

Subjective models are prescriptive approaches in that they reflect beliefs about the nature of organizations. They can be regarded as "anti-theories" in that they emerged as a reaction to the perceived limitations of the formal models. Although subjective models introduce several important concepts into the theory of educational management, they have four significant weaknesses, which serve to limit their validity:

1. Subjective models are strongly normative in that they reflect the attitudes and beliefs of their supporters. Willower (1980) goes further to describe them as "ideological." "[Phenomenological] perspectives feature major ideological components and their partisans tend to be true believers when promulgating their positions rather than offering them for critical examination and test" (p.7).

   Subjective models comprise a series of principles rather than a coherent body of theory: "Greenfield sets out to destroy the central principles of conventional theory but consistently rejects the idea of proposing a precisely formulated alternative" (Hughes and Bush, 1991, p. 241).

2. Subjective models seem to assume the existence of an organization within which individual behaviour and interpretation occur but there is no clear indication of the nature of the organization. Organizations are perceived to be nothing more than a product of the meanings of their participants. In emphasizing the interpretations of individuals, subjective theorists neglect the institutions within which individuals behave, interact and derive meanings.

3. Subjective theorists imply that meanings are so individual that there may be as many interpretations as people. In practice, though, these meanings tend to cluster into patterns, which do enable participants and observers to make valid generalizations about organizations. "By focussing exclusively on the 'individual' as a theoretical...entity, [Greenfield] precludes analyses of collective enterprises. Social phenomena cannot be reduced solely to 'the individual'" (Ryan, 1988, p. 69-70).
4. Subjective models they provide few guidelines for managerial action. Leaders are expected to acknowledge the individual meanings placed on events by members of organizations. This stance is much less secure than the precepts of the formal model.

The Importance of the Individual

The subjective perspective offers some valuable insights, which act as a corrective to the more rigid features of formal models. The focus on individual interpretations of events is a useful antidote to the uniformity of systems and structural theories. Similarly, the emphasis on individual aims, rather than organizational objectives, is an important contribution to our understanding of schools and colleges.

Subjective models have close links with the emerging, but still weakly defined, notion of post-modern leadership. Leaders need to attend to the multiple voices in their organisations and to develop a "power to," not a "power over," model of leadership. However, as Sackney and Mitchell (2001) note, "we do not see how post-modern leadership...can be undertaken without the active engagement of the school principal" (p. 19). In other words, the subjective approach works only if leaders wish it to work, a fragile basis for any approach to educational leadership.

Greenfield's work has broadened our understanding of educational institutions and exposed the weaknesses of the formal models. However, it is evident that subjective models have supplemented, rather than supplanted, the formal theories Greenfield set out to attack.

AMBIGUITY MODELS

Central Features of Ambiguity Models

Ambiguity models stress uncertainty and unpredictability in organizations. These theories assume that organizational objectives are problematic and that institutions experience difficulty in ordering their priorities. Sub-units are portrayed as relatively autonomous groups, which are connected only loosely with one another and with the institution itself. Decision-making occurs within formal and informal settings where participation is fluid. Ambiguity is a prevalent feature of complex organizations such as schools and is likely to be particularly acute during periods of rapid change (Bush, 2003):

Ambiguity models assume that turbulence and unpredictability are dominant features of organizations. There is no clarity over the objectives of institutions and their processes are not properly understood. Participation in policy making is fluid as members opt in or out of decision opportunities. (p. 134)

Ambiguity models are associated with a group of theorists, mostly from the United States, who developed their ideas in the 1970s. They were dissatisfied with the formal models, which they regarded as inadequate for many organizations, particularly during phases of instability. The most celebrated of the ambiguity perspectives is the "garbage can" model developed by Cohen and March (1986). March (1982) points to the jumbled reality in certain kinds of organization:

Theories of choice underestimate the confusion and complexity surrounding actual decision making. Many things are happening at once; technologies are changing and poorly understood; alliances, preferences, and perceptions are changing; problems, solutions, opportunities, ideas, people, and outcomes are mixed together in a way that makes their interpretation uncertain and their connections unclear. (p. 36)

The data supporting ambiguity models have been drawn largely from educational settings, leading March and Olsen (1976) to assert that "ambiguity is a major feature of decision making in most public and educational organizations" (p. 12).

Ambiguity models have the following major features:

1. There is a lack of clarity about the goals of the organization. Many institutions are thought to have inconsistent and opaque objectives. It may be argued that aims become clear only through the behaviour of members of the organization (Cohen and March, 1986):

   The organization appears to operate on a variety of inconsistent and ill-defined preferences. It can be described better as a loose collection of changing ideas than as a coherent structure. It discovers preferences through action more often than it acts on the basis of preferences. (p. 3)

   Educational institutions are regarded as typical in having no clearly defined objectives. Because teachers work independently for much of their time, they may experience little difficulty in pursuing their own interests. As a result schools and colleges are thought to have no coherent pattern of aims.

2. Ambiguity models assume that organizations have a problematic technology in that their processes are not properly understood. In education it is not clear how students acquire knowledge and skills so the processes of teaching are clouded with doubt and uncertainty. Bell (1980) claims that ambiguity infuses the central functions of schools.

3. Ambiguity theorists argue that organizations are characterized by fragmentation. Schools are divided into groups which have internal coherence based on common values and goals. Links between the groups are more tenuous and unpredictable. Weick (1976) uses the term "loose coupling" to describe relationships between sub-units. "Loose coupling...carries connotations of impermanence, dissolvability, and tacit ness all of which are potentially crucial properties of the 'glue'" (p. 3) that holds organizations together.

   Client-serving bodies, such as schools, fit the loose coupling metaphor much better than, say, car assembly plants where operations are regimented and predictable. The degree of integration required in education is markedly less than in many other settings, allowing fragmentation to develop and persist.

4. Within ambiguity models organizational structure is regarded as problematic. Committees and other formal bodies have rights and responsibilities, which overlap with each other and with the authority assigned to individual managers. The effective power of each element within the structure varies with the issue and according to the level of participation of committee members.

5. Ambiguity models tend to be particularly appropriate for professional client-serving organizations. The requirement that professionals make individual judgements, rather than acting in accordance with managerial prescriptions, leads to the view that the larger schools and colleges operate in a climate of ambiguity.

6. Ambiguity theorists emphasize that there is fluid participation in the management of organizations. "The participants in the organization vary among themselves in the amount of time and effort they

devote to the organization; individual participants vary from one time to another. As a result standard theories of power and choice seem to be inadequate." (Cohen and March, 1986, p. 3).

7. A further source of ambiguity is provided by the signals emanating from the organization's environment. In an era of rapid change, schools may experience difficulties in interpreting the various messages being transmitted from the environment and in dealing with conflicting signals. The uncertainty arising from the external context adds to the ambiguity of the decision-making process within the institution.
8. Ambiguity theorists emphasize the prevalence of unplanned decisions. The lack of agreed goals means that decisions have no clear focus. Problems, solutions and participants interact and choices somehow emerge from the confusion.

   The rational model is undermined by ambiguity, since it is so heavily dependent on the availability of information about relationships between inputs and outputs—between means and ends. If ambiguity prevails, then it is not possible for organizations to have clear aims and objectives. (Levacic, 1995, p. 82)
9. Ambiguity models stress the advantages of decentralization. Given the complexity and unpredictability of organizations, it is thought that many decisions should be devolved to subunits and individuals. Weick (1976) argues that devolution enables organizations to survive while particular subunits are threatened (Bush, 2003):

If there is a breakdown in one portion of a loosely coupled system then this breakdown is sealed off and does not affect other portions of the organization . . . A loosely coupled system can isolate its trouble spots and prevent the trouble from spreading. (p. 135-141)

The major contribution of the ambiguity model is that it uncouples problems and choices. The notion of decision-making as a rational process for finding solutions to problems is supplanted by an uneasy mix of problems, solutions and participants from which decisions may eventually emerge. "In the garbage can model, there is no clear distinction between means and ends, no articulation of organizational goals, no evaluation of alternatives in relation to organizational goals and no selection of the best means" (Levacic, 1995, p. 82).

Contingent Leadership

In a climate of ambiguity, traditional notions of leadership require modification. The contingent model provides an alternative approach, recognizing the diverse nature of school contexts and the advantages of adapting leadership styles to the particular situation, rather than adopting a "one size fits all" stance. Yukl (2002) claims that "the managerial job is too complex and unpredictable to rely on a set of standardised responses to events. Effective leaders are continuously reading the situation and evaluating how to adapt their behaviour to it" (p. 234). Contingent leadership depends on managers "mastering a large repertoire of leadership practices" (Leithwood, Jantzi, and Steinbach, 1999, p. 15).

The Limitations of Ambiguity Models

Ambiguity models add some important dimensions to the theory of educational management. The concepts of problematic goals, unclear technology and fluid participation are significant contributions to organizational analysis. Most schools and colleges possess these features to a greater or lesser extent, so ambiguity models should be regarded primarily as analytical or descriptive approaches rather than normative theories. The ambiguity model appears to be increasingly plausible but it does have four significant weaknesses:

1. It is difficult to reconcile ambiguity perspectives with the customary structures and processes of schools and colleges. Participants may move in and out of decision-making situations but the policy framework remains intact and has a continuing influence on the outcome of discussions. Specific goals may be unclear but teachers usually understand and accept the broad aims of education.
2. Ambiguity models exaggerate the degree of uncertainty in educational institutions. Schools and colleges have a number of predictable features, which serve to clarify the responsibilities of their members. Students and staff are expected to behave in accordance with standard rules and procedures. The timetable regulates the location and movement of all participants. There are usually clear plans to guide the classroom activities of teachers and pupils. Staffs are aware of the accountability patterns, with teachers responsible ultimately to principals who, in turn, are answerable to local or State government.

   Educational institutions are rather more stable and predictable than the ambiguity perspective suggests: "The term organised anarchy may seem overly colourful, suggesting more confusion, disarray, and conflict than is really present" (Baldridge et al, 1978, p. 28).
3. Ambiguity models are less appropriate for stable organizations or for any institutions during periods of stability. The degree of predictability in schools depends on the nature of relationships with the external environment. Where institutions are able to maintain relatively impervious boundaries, they can exert strong control over their own processes. Popular schools, for example, may be able to insulate their activities from external pressures.

4. Ambiguity models offer little practical guidance to leaders in educational institutions. While formal models emphasize the head's leading role in policy-making and collegial models stress the importance of team-work, ambiguity models can offer nothing more tangible than contingent leadership.

Ambiguity or Rationality?

Ambiguity models make a valuable contribution to the theory of educational management. The emphasis on the unpredictability of organizations is a significant counter to the view that problems can be solved through a rational process. The notion of leaders making a considered choice from a range of alternatives depends crucially on their ability to predict the consequences of a particular action. The edifice of the formal models is shaken by the recognition that conditions in schools may be too uncertain to allow an informed choice among alternatives.

In practice, however, educational institutions operate with a mix of rational and anarchic processes. The more unpredictable the internal and external environment, the more applicable is the ambiguity metaphor: "Organizations...are probably more rational than they are adventitious and the quest for rational procedures is not misplaced. However,...rationalistic approaches will always be blown off course by the contingent, the unexpected and the irrational" (Hoyle, 1986, p. 72).

CULTURAL MODELS

What Do We Mean By Culture?

Cultural models emphasize the informal aspects of organizations rather then their official elements. They focus on the values, beliefs and norms of individuals in the organization and how these individual perceptions coalesce into shared organizational meanings. Cultural models are manifested by symbols and rituals rather than through the formal structure of the organization (Bush, 2003):

Cultural models assume that beliefs, values and ideology are at the heart of organizations. Individuals hold certain idea and vale-preferences, which influence how they behave and how they view the behaviour of other members. These norms become shared traditions, which are communicated within the group and are reinforced by symbols and ritual. (p. 156).

Beare, Caldwell, and Millikan (1992) claim that culture serves to define the unique qualities of individual organizations: "An increasing number of...writers...have adopted the term "culture" to define that social and phenomenological uniqueness of a particular organisational community...We have finally acknowledged publicly that uniqueness is a virtue, that values are important and that they should be fostered" (p. 173).

Societal Culture

Most of the literature on culture in education relates to organizational culture and that is also the main focus of this section. However, there is also an emerging literature on the broader theme of national or societal culture. Walker and Dimmock (2002) refer to issues of context and stress the need to avoid "decontextualized paradigms" (p. 1) in researching and analyzing educational systems and institutions.

Dimmock and Walker (2002) provide a helpful distinction between societal and organizational culture:

Societal cultures differ mostly at the level of basic values, while organizational cultures differ mostly at the level of more superficial practices, as reflected in the recognition of particular symbols, heroes and rituals. This allows organizational cultures to be deliberately managed and changed, whereas societal or national cultures are more enduring and change only gradually over longer time periods. (p.71)

Societal culture is one important aspect of the context within which school leaders must operate. They must also contend with organizational culture, which provides a more immediate framework for leadership action.

Central Features of Organizational Culture

It focuses on the values and beliefs of members of organizations. "Shared values, shared beliefs, shared meaning, shared understanding, and shared sense making are all different ways of describing culture...These patterns of understanding also provide a basis for making one's own behaviour sensible and meaningful" (Morgan, 1997, p. 138).

The cultural model focuses on the notion of a single or dominant culture in organizations but this does not necessarily mean that individual values are always in harmony with one another. "There may be different and competing value systems that create a mosaic of organizational realities rather than a uniform corporate culture" (Morgan, 1997, p. 137). Large, multipurpose organizations, in particular, are likely to have more than one culture (Schein, 1997, p. 14).

Organizational culture emphasizes the development of shared norms and meanings. The assumption is that interaction between members of the organization, or its subgroups, eventually leads to behavioural norms that gradually become cultural features of the school or college.

These group norms sometimes allow the development of a monoculture in a school with meanings shared throughout the staff - "the way we do things around here." We have already noted, however, that there may be several subcultures based on the professional and personal interests of different groups. These typically have internal coherence but experience difficulty in relationships with other groups whose behavioural norms are different.

Culture is typically expressed through rituals and ceremonies, which are used to support and celebrate beliefs and norms. Schools are rich in such symbols as assemblies, prize-giving and corporate worship. "Symbols are central to the process of constructing meaning." (Hoyle, 1986, p. 152).

Organizational culture assumes the existence of heroes and heroines who embody the values and beliefs of the organization. These honoured members typify the behaviours associated with the culture of the institution. Campbell-Evans (1993, p. 106) stresses that heroes or heroines are those whose achievements match the culture: "Choice and recognition of heroes...occurs within the cultural boundaries identified through the value filter...The accomplishments of those individuals who come to be regarded as heroes are compatible with the cultural emphases" (Bush, 2003, p. 160-162).

Moral Leadership

Leaders have the main responsibility for generating and sustaining culture and communicating core values and beliefs both within the organization and to external stakeholders (Bush, 1998, p. 43). Principals have their own values and beliefs arising from many years of successful professional practice. They are also expected to embody the culture of the school or college. Schein (1997) argues that cultures spring primarily from the beliefs, values and assumptions of founders of organizations. However, it should be noted that cultural change is difficult and problematic. Hargreaves (1999) claims that "most people's beliefs, attitudes and values are far more resistant to change than leaders typically allow" (p. 59-60).

The leadership model most closely linked to organizational culture is that of moral leadership. This model assumes that the critical focus of leadership ought to be on the values, beliefs and ethics of leaders themselves. Authority and influence are to be derived from defensible conceptions of what is right or good (Leithwood *et al.,* 1999, p. 10).

Sergiovanni (1984) says that "excellent schools have central zones composed of values and beliefs that take on sacred or cultural characteristics" (p. 10). The moral dimension of leadership is based on "normative rationality; rationality based on what we believe and what we consider to be good" (Sergiovanni, 1991):

Moral leadership is consistent with organizational culture in that it is based on the values, beliefs and attitudes of principals and other educational leaders. It focuses on the moral purpose of education and on the behaviours to be expected of leaders operating within the moral domain. It also assumes that these values and beliefs coalesce into shared norms and meanings that either shape or reinforce culture. The rituals and symbols associated with moral leadership support these values and underpin school culture. (p. 326)

Limitations of Organizational Culture

Cultural models add several useful elements to the analysis of school and college leadership and management. The focus on the informal dimension is a valuable counter to the rigid and official components of the formal models. By stressing the values and beliefs of participants, cultural models reinforce the human aspects of management rather than their structural elements. The emphasis on the symbols of the organization is also a valuable contribution to management theory while the moral leadership model provides a useful way of understanding what constitutes a values-based approach to leadership. However, cultural models do have three significant weaknesses:

1. There may be ethical dilemmas because cultural leadership may be regarded as the imposition of a culture by leaders on other members of the organization. The search for a monoculture may mean subordinating the values and beliefs of some participants to those of leaders or the dominant group.

Morgan (1997, p. 150-51) refers to "a process of ideological control" and warns of the risk of "manipulation."

2. The cultural model may be unduly mechanistic, assuming that leaders can determine the culture of the organization (Morgan, 1997). While they have influence over the evolution of culture by espousing desired values, they cannot ensure the emergence of a monoculture. As we have seen, secondary schools and colleges may have several subcultures operating in departments and other sections. This is not necessarily dysfunctional because successful subunits are vital components of thriving institutions.
3. The cultural model's focus on symbols such as rituals and ceremonies may mean that other elements of organizations are underestimated. The symbols may misrepresent the reality of the school or college. Hoyle (1986, p. 166) refers to "innovation without change." Schools may go through the appearance of change but the reality continues as before.

Values and Action

The cultural model is a valuable addition to our understanding of organizations. The recognition that school and college development needs to be preceded by attitudinal change is salutary, and consistent with the maxim that teachers must feel "ownership" of change if it is to be implemented effectively. "Since organization ultimately resides in the heads of the people involved, effective organizational change always implies cultural change" (Morgan, 1997, p. 150).

Cultural models also provide a focus for organizational action, a dimension that is largely absent from the subjective perspective. Leaders may adopt a moral approach and focus on influencing values so that they become closer to, if not identical with, their own beliefs. In this way, they hope to achieve widespread support for or "ownership" of new policies. By working through this informal domain, rather than imposing change through positional authority or political processes, heads and principals are more likely to gain support for innovation. An appreciation of organizational culture is an important element in the leadership and management of schools and colleges.

CONCLUSION

Comparing the Management Models

The six management models discussed in this chapter represent different ways of looking at educational institutions. Each screen offers valuable insights into the nature of management in education but none provides a complete picture. The six approaches are all valid analyses but their relevance varies according to the context. Each event, situation or problem may be understood by using one or more of these models but no organization can be explained by using only a single approach. There is no single perspective capable of presenting a total framework for our understanding of educational institutions. "The search for an all-encompassing model is simplistic, for no one model can delineate the intricacies of decision processes in complex organizations such as universities and colleges" (Baldridge et al, 1978, p. 28).

The formal models dominated the early stages of theory development in educational management. Formal structure, rational decision-making and "top-down" leadership were regarded as the central concepts of effective management and attention was given to refining these processes to increase efficiency. Since the 1970s, however, there has been a gradual realization that formal models are "at best partial and at worst grossly deficient" (Chapman, 1993, p. 215).

The other five models featured in this volume all developed in response to the perceived weaknesses of what was then regarded as "conventional theory." They have demonstrated the limitations of the formal models and put in place alternative conceptualizations of school management. While these more recent models are all valid, they are just as partial as the dominant perspective their advocates seek to replace. There is more theory and, by exploring different dimensions of management, its total explanatory power is greater than that provided by any single model.

Collegial models are attractive because they advocate teacher participation in decision-making. Many principals aspire to collegiality, a claim that rarely survives rigorous scrutiny. The collegial framework all too often provides the setting for political activity or "top-down" decision-making (Bush, 2003).

The cultural model's stress on values and beliefs, and the subjective theorists' emphasis on the significance of individual meanings, also appear to be both plausible and ethical. In practice, however, these may lead to manipulation as leaders seek to impose their own values on schools and colleges.

The increasing complexity of the educational context may appear to lend support to the ambiguity model with its emphasis on turbulence and anarchy. However, this approach provides few guidelines for managerial action and leads to the view that "there has to be a better way."

The six models differ along crucial dimensions but taken together they do provide a comprehensive picture of the nature of management in educational institutions.

Attempts at Synthesis

Each of the models discussed in this volume offers valid insights into the nature of leadership and management in schools and colleges. Yet all the perspectives are limited in that they do not give a complete picture of educational

Elements of management	Formal	Collegial	Political	Subjective	Ambiguity	Cultural
Level at which goals are determined	Institutional	Institutional	Sub-unit	Individual	Unclear	Institutional or sub-unit
Process by which goals are determined	Set by leaders	Agreement	Conflict	Problematic may be imposed by leaders	Unpredictable	Based on collective value
Relationship between goals and decisions	Decisions based on goals	Decisions based on agreed goals	Decision based on goals of dominant coalitions	Individual behaviour based on personal goals	Decisions unrelated to goals	Decision based on the goals of the organiation or its sub-units
Nature of decision process	Rational	Collegial	Political	Personal	Garbage can	Rational within a framework of values
Nature of structure	Objective reality Hierarchical	objective reality Lateral	Setting for sub-unit activity	Constructed through human interaction	Problematic	Physical manifestation of culture

Elements of management	Formal	Collegial	Political	Subjective	Ambiguity	Cultural
Links with environment	May be "closed" or "open" Principal accountable	Accountability blurred by shared decision-making	Unstable external bodies portrayed as interest groups	Source of individual meanings	Source of uncertainty	Source of values and beliefs
Style of Leadership	Principal establishes goals and initiates policy	Principal seeks to promote consensus	Principal is both participant and mediator	Problematic May be perceived as a form of control	May be tactical or unobtrusive	Symbolic
Related leadership model	Managerial	Participative	Transactional	Post-modem	Contingent	Moral

Fig. 13.2. Compares the main features of the six models

institutions. "Organizations are many things at once! They are complex and multifaceted. They are paradoxical. That's why the challenges facing management are so difficult. In any given situation there may be many different tendencies and dimensions, all of which have an impact on effective management" (Morgan, 1997, p. 347).

The inadequacies of each theory, taken singly, have led to a search for a comprehensive model that integrates concepts to provide a coherent analytical framework. Chapman (1993) stresses the need for leaders to develop this broader perspective in order to enhance organizational effectiveness: "Visionary and creative leadership and effective management in education require a deliberate and conscious attempt at integration, enmeshment and coherence" (p. 212).

Enderud (1980), and Davies and Morgan (1983), have developed integrative models incorporating ambiguity, political, collegial and formal perspectives. These syntheses are based on the assumption that policy formation proceeds through four distinct phases which all require adequate time if the decision is to be successful. These authors assume an initial period of high ambiguity as problems, solutions and participants interact at appropriate choice opportunities. This anarchic phase serves to identify the issues and acts as a preliminary sifting mechanism. If conducted properly it should lead to an initial coupling of problems with potential solutions.

The output of the ambiguous period is regarded as the input to the political phase. This stage is characterized by bargaining and negotiations and usually involves relatively few participants in small, closed committees. The outcome is likely to be a broad measure of agreement on possible solutions.

In the third collegial phase, the participants committed to the proposed solution attempt to persuade less active members to accept the compromise reached during the political stage. The solutions are tested against criteria of acceptability and feasibility and may result in minor changes. Eventually this process should lead to agreed policy outcomes and a degree of commitment to the decision.

The final phase is the formal or bureaucratic stage during which agreed policy may be subject to modification in the light of administrative considerations. The outcome of this period is a policy which is both legitimate and operationally satisfactory (Bush, 2003, p. 193).

Theodossin (1983, p. 88) links the subjective to the formal or systems model using an analytical continuum. He argues that a systems perspective is the most appropriate way of explaining national developments while individual and subunit activities may be understood best by utilizing the individual meanings of participants:

Theodossin's analysis is interesting and plausible. It helps to delineate the contribution of the formal and subjective models to educational management theory. In focusing on these two perspectives, however, it necessarily ignores the contribution of other approaches, including the cultural model, which has not been incorporated into any of the syntheses applied to education

The Enderud (1980), and Davies and Morgan (1983), models are valuable in suggesting a plausible sequential link between four of the major theories. However, it is certainly possible to postulate different sets of relationships between the models. For example, a collegial approach may become political as participants engage in conflict instead of seeking to achieve consensus. It is perhaps significant that there have been few attempts to integrate the management models since the 1980s.

Using Theory to Improve Practice

The six models present different approaches to the management of education and the syntheses indicate a few of the possible relationships between them. However, the ultimate test of theory is whether it improves practice. There should be little doubt about the potential for theory to inform practice. School managers generally engage in a process of implicit theorising in deciding how to formulate policy or respond to events. Facts cannot be left to speak for themselves. They require the explanatory framework of theory in order to ascertain their real meaning.

The multiplicity of competing models means that no single theory is sufficient to guide practice. Rather, managers need to develop "conceptual pluralism" (Bolman and Deal, 1984, p. 4) to be able to select the most appropriate approach to particular issues and avoid a unidimensional stance: "Managers in all organizations...can increase their effectiveness and their freedom through the use of multiple vantage points. To be locked into a single path is likely to produce error and self-imprisonment" (p. 4).

Conceptual pluralism is similar to the notion of contingent leadership. Both recognize the diverse nature of educational contexts and the advantages of adapting leadership styles to the particular situation rather than adopting a "one size fits all" stance. Appreciation of the various models is the starting point for effective action. It provides a "conceptual tool-kit" for the manager to deploy as appropriate in addressing problems and developing strategy.

Morgan (1997, p. 359) argues that organizational analysis based on these multiple perspectives comprises two elements:

- A diagnostic reading of the situation being investigated, using different metaphors to identify or highlight key aspects of the situation.
- A critical evaluation of the significance of the different interpretations resulting from the diagnosis.

These skills are consistent with the concept of the "reflective practitioner" whose managerial approach incorporates both good experience and a distillation of theoretical models based on wide reading and discussion with both academics and fellow practitioners. This combination of theory and practice enables the leader to acquire the overview required for strategic management.

While it is widely recognized that appreciation of theory is likely to enhance practice, there remain relatively few published accounts of how the various models have been tested in school or college-based research. More empirical work is needed to enable judgements on the validity of the models to be made with confidence. The objectives of such a research programme would be to test the validity of the models presented in this volume and to develop an overarching conceptual framework. It is a tough task but if awareness of theory helps to improve practice, as we have sought to demonstrate, then more rigorous theory should produce more effective practitioners and better schools.

REFERENCES

1. Baldridge, J. V. (1971). Power and Conflict in the University. New York: John Wiley.
2. Baldridge, J. V., Curtis, D. V., Ecker, G. and Riley, G. L. (1978). Policy-making and Effective Leadership. San Francisco: Jossey Bass.
3. Ball, S. (1987). The Micropolitics of the School: Towards a Theory of School Organization. London: Methuen.
4. Beare, H., Caldwell, B., and Millikan, R. (1992). Creating an Excellent School. London: Routledge.
5. Bell, L. (1980). The School as an Organisation: A Re-appraisal. British Journal of Sociology of Education, 1(2), 183-92.
6. Bolman, L. and Deal, T. (1984). Modern Approaches to Understanding and Managing Organizations. San Francisco: Jossey Bass.
7. Bolman, L.G. and Deal, T.E. (1991, 1997). Reframing Organizations: Artistry, Choice and Leadership. an Francisco: Jossey Bass
8. Brundrett, M. (1998). What Lies Behind Collegiality, Legitimation or Control? Educational Management and Administration, 26(3), 305-316.

9. Bush, T. (1986). Theories of Educational Management. London: Harper and Row.
10. Bush, T. (1995). Theories of Educational Management: Second Edition. London: Paul Chapman.
11. Bush, T. (1998). Organisational Culture and Strategic Management. In D. Middle Wood and J. Lumby (Eds.), Strategic Management in Schools and Colleges. London: Paul Chapman.
12. Bush, T. (1999). Crisis or Crossroads? The Discipline of Educational Management in the Late 1990s. Educational Management and Administration, 27(3), 239-252.
13. Bush, T. (2003). Theories of Educational Management: Third Edition. London: Sage.
14. Bush, T. (2006). The National College for School Leadership: A Successful English Innovation, Phi Delta Kappan, 87(7), 508-511.
15. Bush, T. and Glover, D. (2002). School Leadership: Concepts and Evidence. Nottingham: National College for School Leadership.
16. Campbell-Evans, G. (1993). A Values Perspective on School-based Management. In C. Dimmock (Ed.), School-based Management and School Effectiveness. London: Routledge.
17. Chapman, J. (1993). Leadership, School-based Decision-making and School Effectiveness. In C. Dimmock (Ed.). School-based Management and School Effectiveness. London: Routledge.
18. Cohen, L., Manion, L. & Morrison, K. (2000). Research Methods in Education (5th Ed.). Routledge Falmer: London.
19. Cohen, M. D. and March, J. G. (1986). Leadership and Ambiguity: The American College President. Boston: The Harvard Business School Press.
20. Copland, M., Darling-Hammond, L., Knapp, M., McLaugghlin, M. & Talbert, J. (2002). Leadership for Teaching and Learning: A Framework for Research and Action. New Orleans: American Educational Research Association.
21. Cuban, L. (1988). The Managerial Imperative and the Practice of Leadership in Schools. Albany, NY: State University of New York Press.
22. Davies, J.L. and Morgan, A. W. (1983). Management of Higher Education in a Period of Contraction and Uncertainty. In O. Body-Barrett, T. Bush, J. Goodey, J. McNay & M. Preedy (Eds.). Approaches to Post School Management. London: Harper and Row.

23. Dimmock, C. (1999). Principals and School Restructuring: Conceptualising Challenges as Dilemmas. Journal of Educational Administration, 37(5), 441-462.

24. Dimmock, C. & Walker, A. (2002b). School Leadership in Context—Societal and Organizational Cultures. In T. Bush and L. Bell (Eds.). The Principles and Practice of Educational Management. London: Paul Chapman.

25. Dressler, B. (2001). Charter School Leadership. Education and Urban Society, 33(2), 170-185.

26. Enderud, H. (1980) Administrative Leadership in Organised Anarchies, International Journal of Institutional Management in Higher Education, 4(3), 235-53.

27. English, F. (2002). Cutting the Gordian Knot of Educational Administration: The Theory-practice Gap, The Review, XLIV (1), 1-3.

28. Glaser, B. G. and Strauss, A. L. (1967). The Discovery of Grounded Theory, Weidenfeld and Nicolson, London.

29. Greenfield, T. B. (1973). Organisations as Social Inventions: Rethinking Assumptions About Change, Journal of Applied Behavioural Science, 9: 5, 551-74.

30. Greenfield, T. B. (1975). Theory About Organisations: A New Perspective and Its Implications for Schools, in M. Hughes (Ed.) Administering Education: International Challenge, Athlone Press, London.

31. Greenfield, T. B. (1979). Organisation Theory is Ideology, Curriculum Enquiry, 9: 2, 97-112.

32. Griffiths, D. (1997). The Case for Theoretical Pluralism, Educational Management and Administration, 25 (4), 371-380

33. Handy, C. (1993). Understanding Organizations, Penguin, London.

34. Hargreaves, A. (1994). Changing Teachers, Changing Times: Teachers" Work and Culture in the Postmodern Age, Cassell, London.

35. Hargreaves, D. (1999). Helping Practitioners Explore Their School's culture, in J. Prosser (Ed.). School Culture, Paul Chapman, London.

36. Hodgkinson, C. (1993). Foreword, in T. B. Greenfield and P. Ribbins (eds.). Greenfield on Educational Administration, Routledge, London.

37. Hoyle, E. (1986). The Politics of School Management, Hodder and Stoughton, Sevenoaks.
38. Keough, T. and Tobin, B. (2001). Postmodern Leadership and the Policy Lexicon: From Theory, Proxy to Practice, Paper for the Pan-Canadian Education Research Agenda Symposium, Quebec, May.
39. Leithwood, K., Jantzi, D. and Steinbach, R. (1999). Changing Leadership for Changing Times. Buckingham: Open University Press.
40. Levacic, R. (1995). Local Management of Schools: Analysis and Practice, Open University Press, Buckingham.
41. Levacic, R., Glover, D., Bennett, N. and Crawford, M. (1999). Modern Headship for the Rationally Managed School: Combining Cerebral and Insightful Approaches, in T. Bush and L. Bell (Eds.). The Principles and Practice of Educational Management, Paul Chapman, London.
42. Lindle, J. (1999). What Can the Study of Micropolitics Contribute to the Practice of Leadership in Reforming Schools, School Leadership and Management, Vol.19, No.2, pp.171-178.
43. Little, J. (1990). Teachers as Colleagues, in A. Lieberman (ed.). Schools as Collaborative Cultures: Creating the Future Now, The Falmer Press, Basingstoke.
44. March, J. G. (1982). Theories of Choice and Making Decisions, Society, Vol. 20, No. 1, Copyright © by Transaction Inc. Published by Permission of Transaction Inc.
45. March, J. G. and Olsen, J. P. (1976). Organisational Choice Under Ambiguity, in J. G. March and J. P. Olsen, Ambiguity and Choice in Organisations, Universitetsforlaget, Bergen.
46. Miller, T.W. and Miller, J.M. (2001). Educational Leadership in the New Millennium: A Vision for 2020, International Journal of Leadership in Education, 4 (2), 181-189.
47. Morgan, G. (1997). Images of Organization, Sage, Newbury Park, California.
48. Morrison, M. (2002). What Do We Mean by Educational Research?, in M. Coleman and A. Briggs (Eds.). Research Methods in Educational Leadership and Management, Paul Chapman, London.
49. Newman, J. and Clarke, J. (1994). Going About Our Business? The Managerialism of Public Services, in Clarke, J., Cochrane, A. and McLaughlin, E. (Eds.). Managing School Policy, London, Sage.
50. Owens, R. and Shakeshaft, C. (1992). The New "Revolution" in Administrative Theory, Journal of Educational Management, 30: 9, 4-17.

51. Ribbins, P. (1985). Organisation theory and the Study of Educational Institutions, in M. Hughes, P. Ribbins and H. Thomas (eds.). Managing Education: The System and the Institution, Holt, Rinehart and Winston, London.
52. Ryan, J. (1988). Science in Educational Administration: A Comment on the Holmes-Greenfield dialogue, Interchange, 19: 2, 68-70, Summer.
53. Sackney, L. and Mitchell, C. (2001). Postmodern Expressions of Educational Leadership, in K. Leithwood and P. Hallinger (Eds.). The Second International Handbook of Educational Leadership and Administration, Kluwer, Dordrecht.
54. Samier, E. (2002), Weber on Education and Its Administration: Prospects for Leadership in a Rationalised World, Educational Management and Administration, 30(1), 27-45.
55. Schein, E. (1997). Organizational Culture and Leadership, Jossey Bass, San Francisco.
56. Sergiovanni, T. (1984). Leadership and Excellence in Schooling, Educational Leadership, 41(5), 4-13.
57. Sergiovanni, T.J. (1991). The Principalship: A Reflective Practice Perspective, Needham Heights, MA, Allyn and Bacon.
58. Simkins, T. (1999). Values, Power and Instrumentality: Theory and Research in Education Management, Educational Management and Administration, 27 (3), 267-281.
59. Theodossin, E. (1983). Theoretical Perspectives on the Management of Planned Educational Change, British Education Research Journal, 9 (1),81-90.
60. Walker, A. and Dimmock, C. (2002). Introduction, in Walker, A. and Dimmock, C. (Eds.). School Leadership and Administration: Adopting a Cultural Perspective,Routledge Falmer, London.
61. Wallace, M. (1989). Towards a Collegiate Approach to Curriculum Management in Primary and Middle Schools, in M. Preedy (ed.). Approaches to Curriculum Management, Open University Press, Milton Keynes.
62. Webb, R. & Vulliamy, G. (1996). A Deluge of Directives: Conflict Between Collegiality and Managerialism in the Post-ERA Primary School, British Educational Research Journal,22 : 4, 441-458.
63. Weick, K. E. (1976). Educational Organisations as Loosely Coupled Systems, Administrative Science Quarterly, 21: 1, 1-19.
64. Willower, D. J. (1980). Contemporary Issues in Theory in Educational Administration, Educational Administration Quarterly, 16: 3, 1-25.
65. Yukl, G. A. (2002). Leadership in Organizations, Fifth Edition, Upper Saddle River, NJ, Prentice-Hall.

Index

D

E

❑❑❑